The 12 Days of Financial Freedom

The 12 Days of Financial Freedom

Matthew Petchinsky

CONTENTS

Let's Save Money!

The 12 Days of Financial Freedom: A Step-by-Step Christmas Countdown to Transform Your Finances
By: Matthew Petchinsky

Introduction: A Christmas Gift for Your Financial Future

The holiday season, for many, is a time of joy, celebration, and togetherness. But it can also bring an overwhelming sense of financial pressure. The expectations to give lavish gifts, host parties, decorate homes, and travel to visit loved ones often leave people feeling drained—both emotionally and financially. The financial stress that peaks during the holidays can overshadow the true spirit of Christmas, leaving you with lingering debt and an empty wallet as the new year rolls in. This book, **"The 12 Days of Financial Freedom,"** is designed to change that narrative, giving you not only relief from holiday financial strain but also the tools to set yourself up for financial success well into the future.

Setting the Stage: Why Financial Stress Peaks During the Holidays and How This Book Can Help You Gain Control Over Your Finances

The holidays are notorious for amplifying financial stress for a number of reasons:

1. **Pressure to Spend**: Whether it's on gifts, food, or travel, holiday spending can spiral out of control quickly. Many people feel obligated to spend beyond their means to meet the expectations of friends and family, often turning to credit cards and accruing debt.

2. **Unexpected Expenses**: There are always those last-minute purchases—forgotten gifts, extra party supplies, or surprise travel costs. These unexpected expenses add up, often wreaking havoc on an already stretched budget.

3. **End-of-Year Financial Fatigue**: After a long year of managing expenses, savings, and debt, many people feel burnt out and unprepared to handle the holiday splurge. Financial fatigue often leads to poor decision-making during the holidays.

4. **New Year on the Horizon**: With the new year approaching, thoughts of financial resolutions begin to surface, yet many are too overwhelmed by their current financial state to set clear goals for the future.

This book is here to help you tackle all of these challenges head-on. **"The 12 Days of Financial Freedom"** offers practical, actionable steps to help you regain control over your finances, just in time for the holidays. By following the 12-day plan outlined in this book, you'll not only reduce your holiday financial stress, but you'll also set yourself up for a financially prosperous new year.

The Promise of Transformation: What Financial Freedom Looks Like and How This 12-Day Plan Can Give You the Tools to Achieve It

Imagine waking up on Christmas morning without the cloud of financial worry hanging over your head. Instead of feeling anxious about bills, credit card debt, or overspending, you feel empowered, knowing you have a clear handle on your finances. That's what financial freedom looks like: the ability to make confident financial decisions, free from the burden of debt and the anxiety of scarcity.

Financial freedom isn't just about being debt-free or having a certain amount of money in the bank—it's about having control over your financial future, making intentional choices that align with your goals, and feeling secure in your ability to handle unexpected challenges. This 12-day plan provides the tools to achieve that freedom. Over the course of 12 days, you'll:

- Create a realistic and manageable holiday budget, so you can enjoy the season without guilt or stress.
- Identify and clarify your financial goals for the new year, setting the foundation for long-term success.
- Learn powerful strategies for paying off debt, saving more effectively, and building a secure financial future.
- Master the art of mindful spending, ensuring that every dollar you spend during the holidays serves a purpose.
- Explore passive income opportunities, tax benefits, and investment strategies that can grow your wealth.

By the end of the 12 days, you will have not only survived the holiday season but also positioned yourself for a financially sound and prosperous new year. This transformation starts with a single step: committing to these 12 days of financial empowerment.

How to Use This Book: Guidelines on Completing the Exercises, Setting Aside Daily Time, and Tracking Your Progress

This book is designed to guide you through a 12-day journey of financial transformation, with each day focusing on a specific area of your financial life. Here's how to get the most out of this book:

1. **Set Aside Daily Time**: To experience the full benefits of this plan, you'll need to dedicate at least 30 minutes to one hour each day to read the day's chapter, complete the exercises, and reflect on your progress. Early morning or late evening is often the best time for this reflection, but choose a time that works best for your schedule and stick to it consistently.

2. **Complete the Exercises**: Each chapter includes interactive exercises designed to help you apply what you've learned. These are not just theoretical activities—they are practical steps that will lead to real changes in your financial life. Completing these exercises is crucial to achieving the transformation you seek.

3. **Track Your Progress**: Use the provided worksheets and tracking tools to monitor your progress throughout the 12 days. Whether it's reducing debt, creating a budget, or setting financial goals, keeping track of your efforts will help you stay motivated and ensure you are making progress toward your financial freedom.

4. **Reflect on Your Journey**: At the end of each day, take a moment to reflect on what you've learned and how you feel about your progress. Journaling your thoughts and experiences can deepen your understanding of your relationship with money and help you see the impact of the changes you're making.

5. **Stay Committed**: It's important to stay committed throughout the 12 days. Financial transformation doesn't happen overnight, but by dedicating time and effort each day, you'll be amazed at how much progress you can make.

Why Christmas is the Perfect Time for Financial Change: Leveraging the Holidays to Set Yourself Up for Long-Term Financial Success

You might be thinking that Christmas—the season of spending and giving—is an odd time to embark on a financial transformation journey. But in fact, the holidays present a unique opportunity for financial change:

1. **A Time for Reflection**: The end of the year naturally invites self-reflection. As you think about what went well and what didn't over the past year, it's the perfect time to assess your financial habits and make changes that will set you up for success in the new year.

2. **The Pressure to Spend**: The holiday spending frenzy can reveal a lot about your relationship with money. By confronting these challenges during the most financially stressful time of the year, you can build lasting financial habits that will carry you through less intense times.

3. **Setting New Year's Financial Goals**: As the new year approaches, you have a clean slate to set new financial goals. Starting during the holidays allows you to begin the new year with a clear plan and positive momentum.

4. **Creating Joy Without Financial Stress**: The holidays are meant to be a time of joy, but financial worries can rob you of that joy. By taking control of your finances now, you'll experience more freedom to fully enjoy the season without the burden of debt or overspending.

5. **Starting the New Year Ahead**: Many people wait until January to set financial resolutions, but by starting now, you'll be ahead of the game. You'll enter the new year with a clear financial plan, a budget in place, and perhaps even some savings from the holiday season.

Christmas is a time of giving, and this book is a gift to yourself—one that will keep on giving long after the holidays are over. By following the 12-day plan, you'll gain the tools, knowledge, and confidence to not only navigate the holidays without financial stress but also set yourself up for a lifetime of financial freedom.

This Christmas, take control of your financial future and give yourself the best gift of all—financial peace of mind.

Chapter 1: Day 1 – The Christmas Budget Miracle

The holidays are a magical time of the year, but they can also be financially overwhelming. Many of us get caught up in the excitement and festivities, only to realize too late that we've overspent on gifts, food, entertainment, and travel. If you're like most people, January can bring the unwelcome realization that the joy of December has turned into a mountain of debt and financial stress.

This chapter is about avoiding that dreaded post-holiday financial hangover by taking control of your holiday spending from day one. By understanding your current spending habits and creating a budget that balances festive fun with financial responsibility, you'll set yourself up for success not just for this holiday season, but for many more to come.

Understanding Your Holiday Spending: Evaluate Your Current Spending Habits for Gifts, Food, and Entertainment

The first step toward a financially stress-free Christmas is gaining a clear understanding of where your money is currently going. Holiday spending often creeps up on us—we justify an extra gift here, a few more decorations there, and before we know it, the credit card bill is higher than expected. It's easy to get swept up in the season, but now is the time to pause and assess your true holiday expenses.

Identifying Common Spending Areas

Holiday spending generally falls into a few major categories:

1. **Gifts**: This is often the largest portion of holiday spending. From immediate family and close friends to co-workers and neighbors, the list of people you feel obligated to buy gifts for can grow quickly.

2. **Food and Entertainment**: The holiday season brings gatherings, parties, and feasts. Whether you're hosting Christmas dinner, attending holiday parties, or simply stocking up on festive treats, food and entertainment costs can add up fast.

3. **Decorations**: Many people love to make their homes look festive, with lights, ornaments, and other seasonal decorations. While beautiful, these can become a significant expense if not managed carefully.

4. **Travel**: If you're visiting family or friends over the holidays, travel expenses can be a big part of your budget. Plane tickets, gas, hotel stays, and even road trip snacks can eat into your holiday funds.

5. **Miscellaneous Holiday Expenses**: This includes everything from holiday cards and postage to charitable donations and winter activities (like ice skating or Christmas markets).

Take a moment to think about how much you've spent in each of these areas in past holiday seasons. Look back at your bank statements or credit card bills from previous years if you need a clearer picture.

Reflecting on Past Holiday Spending

As you evaluate your past spending, ask yourself the following questions:

- Did you overspend last year? If so, in which areas?
- Are there certain expenses that surprised you or caught you off guard?
- Did you use credit to pay for holiday purchases, and are you still paying off that debt?
- Were there any purchases you regretted or felt were unnecessary after the holiday season ended?
- Did you feel financially stressed during or after the holidays?

Understanding your holiday spending habits is the first step to creating a budget that reflects your financial reality and helps you avoid holiday debt.

Creating a Holiday Budget: Learn How to Set a Realistic Budget Without Missing Out on Festive Fun

Now that you have a clear understanding of your holiday spending, it's time to create a realistic holiday budget that ensures you stay in control of your finances without sacrificing the joy and fun of the season. A well-planned budget will help you prioritize what's truly important, avoid unnecessary expenses, and prevent the post-holiday financial strain.

Step 1: Determine How Much You Can Afford

The most important part of budgeting for the holidays is knowing your financial limits. How much can you comfortably afford to spend without dipping into savings or taking on debt? To determine this, you'll need to take a close look at your overall financial situation:

- **Evaluate your income**: Start by calculating your total income for the holiday season. This might include your salary, bonuses, or any other sources of income. Make sure you focus on the disposable income you have after paying necessary bills, such as rent, utilities, and groceries.

- **Assess your existing savings**: If you've set aside money throughout the year specifically for holiday spending, great! Include this in your holiday budget. However, if your savings are meant for other goals (like an emergency fund or a vacation), resist the temptation to dip into those funds for holiday expenses.

- **Check your current financial obligations**: Consider whether you have any large upcoming expenses that might affect your holiday budget, such as property taxes, car repairs, or healthcare costs.

Once you've evaluated your finances, set a firm amount that you can afford to spend for the entire holiday season. This is your overall holiday budget, and everything else you plan should fit within this number.

Step 2: Prioritize Your Holiday Spending

Now that you know your overall budget, it's time to break it down into categories. Start by prioritizing your most important holiday expenses. You can categorize your spending into the following buckets:

1. **Gifts**: Make a list of the people you intend to buy gifts for, and assign a spending limit to each person. Remember, thoughtful gifts don't have to be expensive. Set realistic expectations for what you can afford and consider alternatives like homemade gifts, experiences, or meaningful low-cost items.

2. **Food and Entertainment**: If you're hosting or attending holiday gatherings, estimate how much you'll need to spend on food, drinks, and entertainment. Think about how many people you'll be feeding, whether you'll need to buy extra groceries, or if you'll be eating out during the season.

3. **Decorations**: If you already own holiday decorations, consider reusing them. If you plan to purchase new items, decide how much you want to allocate. Set a strict limit to avoid overspending on festive décor.

4. **Travel**: If you're traveling for the holidays, plan out the cost of transportation, lodging, and any other related expenses. Book tickets early to avoid price hikes and explore budget-friendly travel options.

5. **Miscellaneous Expenses**: Set aside a small portion of your budget for unexpected or last-minute purchases, such as extra holiday cards, an additional gift, or seasonal activities. This buffer will help you avoid blowing your budget if something unplanned comes up.

Step 3: Track Your Spending in Real-Time

To ensure you stick to your budget, it's important to track your spending in real time. You can do this using a simple spreadsheet, budgeting app, or even the personalized holiday budget worksheet provided in this chapter. Each time you make a purchase, record it under the appropriate category. This will help you stay accountable and avoid overspending in one area at the expense of another.

If you notice you're getting close to your spending limit in one category, look for ways to cut back. For example, if your gift budget is running low, consider DIY gifts, or reduce your decoration budget to free up funds for other priorities.

Action Step: Create Your Personalized Holiday Budget Worksheet

To make this process easier and more manageable, you will now create your own **Personalized Holiday Budget Worksheet**. This worksheet will allow you to track your overall holiday spending and ensure that you stay within your set limits.

Steps to Complete Your Worksheet:

1. **Write Down Your Total Holiday Budget**: This is the total amount you've determined you can afford to spend for the holiday season.
2. **List Each Spending Category**: Create sections for each of the following categories:
   - Gifts
   - Food and Entertainment
   - Decorations
   - Travel
   - Miscellaneous Expenses
3. **Assign a Spending Limit to Each Category**: Based on your overall budget, decide how much you can allocate to each category. Be realistic about what you can afford in each area, and prioritize the categories that matter most to you.
4. **Track Your Spending**: As you make purchases, record the amount in the appropriate category. Keep a running total to see how much you've spent so far and how much you have left to spend in each category.
5. **Adjust as Needed**: If you go over in one category, adjust your spending in another category to stay within your overall budget.

By the end of this exercise, you'll have a complete, customized holiday budget that will help you stay financially secure throughout the holiday season. You can find a printable version of the **Personalized Holiday Budget Worksheet** in the appendix.

This first step is all about building awareness and control over your holiday spending. With a clear understanding of your spending habits and a budget that aligns with your financial reality, you'll be able to enjoy the magic of the holidays without the financial stress that usually accompanies it. Remember, financial freedom during the holidays starts with thoughtful planning—and you're well on your way!

Chapter 2: Day 2 – The Gift of Clarity: Identifying Your Financial Goals

One of the most empowering steps in your financial transformation journey is gaining clarity about your financial situation and setting meaningful goals for your future. Without clear goals, managing money can feel like navigating through fog—you might know where you want to go, but without a map or direction, you'll likely get lost or go off course. Day 2 is all about lifting that fog, allowing you to see your financial landscape clearly and chart a path toward financial security and freedom.

In this chapter, you will assess your current financial situation and use that insight to define both short-term and long-term goals. These goals will act as your financial compass, guiding your spending, saving, and investing decisions, and helping you stay on track, even when life gets busy.

Assessing Your Financial Situation: Get Clear on Your Assets, Debts, and Savings

Before you can set effective financial goals, it's crucial to understand exactly where you stand. This involves assessing your assets, liabilities, and overall financial health. Taking stock of your financial situation may seem daunting, but it's a necessary step to establish a solid foundation for your future.

Step 1: Listing Your Assets

Your assets are the things you own that have financial value. These could include:

- **Cash and Savings**: The money you have in your checking accounts, savings accounts, or emergency funds.
- **Investments**: Stocks, bonds, mutual funds, or retirement accounts like a 401(k) or IRA.
- **Property**: The value of your home (if you own one), vehicles, or other significant possessions.
- **Other Assets**: Any valuable collections (like art or antiques), business interests, or anything else that could be sold or converted into cash.

Make a list of all your assets and their current values. If you have any investments, be sure to list their current market value, even if it fluctuates over time. This will give you a complete picture of your financial resources.

Step 2: Calculating Your Debts

Next, list all of your liabilities—your debts and financial obligations. These might include:

- **Credit Card Debt**: Any outstanding balances on your credit cards.
- **Loans**: Personal loans, student loans, auto loans, or mortgages.
- **Other Debts**: Medical bills, unpaid taxes, or any other type of liability.

Write down the total amount you owe for each debt, including interest rates and monthly payments. Understanding the full scope of your liabilities will help you prioritize debt repayment and avoid falling deeper into debt.

Step 3: Reviewing Your Savings and Emergency Fund

In addition to assets and debts, it's important to assess your savings. Do you have a dedicated emergency fund? If so, how much is in it? Most financial experts recommend having 3 to 6 months of living expenses saved in an emergency fund to cover unexpected expenses, like medical bills or car repairs.

- **Evaluate Your Savings Rate**: Are you consistently saving a portion of your income each month? Ideally, you should be saving at least 15-20% of your income, though even small contributions can add up over time.

Once you've compiled all this information, you'll have a much clearer picture of your financial standing. With this knowledge, you can now start setting realistic and meaningful financial goals.

Setting Short-Term and Long-Term Goals: Define Your Financial Goals for the Next Year and Beyond

Now that you've assessed your financial situation, it's time to chart your path forward. Financial goals can be broken down into two categories: short-term goals (things you want to achieve within the next year) and long-term goals (those that may take several years or even decades to accomplish).

Step 1: Defining Short-Term Financial Goals

Short-term goals are specific, achievable goals that you can work on in the near future, typically within the next 12 months. These goals should address your most immediate financial needs and help build momentum toward larger, long-term objectives. Examples of short-term financial goals include:

- **Building or Increasing Your Emergency Fund**: If you don't have an emergency fund, or if it's smaller than you'd like, making this a short-term goal is a smart first step.
- **Paying Off Credit Card Debt**: Reducing or eliminating high-interest debt is another common short-term goal. If you have multiple debts, you might want to focus on paying off the smallest balance first (snowball method) or tackling the one with the highest interest rate (avalanche method).
- **Saving for a Specific Purpose**: You might want to save for an upcoming expense, like a vacation, holiday gifts, or home repairs.

When setting short-term goals, make sure they are **SMART**: Specific, Measurable, Achievable, Relevant, and Time-bound. For example, "Save $1,000 in my emergency fund by June 30" is a SMART goal.

Step 2: Defining Long-Term Financial Goals

Long-term goals are your "big picture" financial dreams, often spanning several years or even decades. These goals require more time and planning, but they're essential for securing your financial future. Some common long-term goals include:

- **Saving for Retirement**: If you haven't already, begin contributing to a retirement account like a 401(k) or IRA. Determine how much you need to save annually to achieve the retirement lifestyle you envision.
- **Paying Off a Mortgage or Student Loans**: Eliminating long-term debt, like a mortgage or student loan, can be a key part of your financial journey. While these debts may take years to repay, setting incremental goals will keep you on track.
- **Building Long-Term Investments**: Investing in the stock market or other assets can help you grow your wealth over time. Setting a goal to increase your investment contributions or reach a specific portfolio value is a good long-term objective.
- **Buying a Home or Starting a Business**: If you have major life goals, such as purchasing a home or launching a business, planning for these long-term financial milestones is critical.

As with short-term goals, long-term goals should also be **SMART**. An example might be, "Save $500,000 for retirement by age 65 by contributing $6,000 annually to my IRA."

Step 3: Aligning Your Goals with Your Values

When setting financial goals, it's important to align them with your values and priorities. Ask yourself:

- **What matters most to me?** Do you value financial security, travel, education, or homeownership? Your goals should reflect your values.
- **How will achieving this goal improve my life?** Each goal should have a clear benefit that motivates you to work toward it. For example, paying off debt might give you peace of mind, while saving for retirement could provide financial freedom in your later years.
- **Is this goal realistic?** Make sure your goals are attainable based on your current financial situation. Overly ambitious goals can be discouraging, while achievable ones keep you motivated.

Action Step: Write Down 3 Short-Term and 3 Long-Term Financial Goals Using the Provided Template

Now that you understand the difference between short-term and long-term goals, it's time to put pen to paper (or fingers to keyboard). Use the following template to write down three short-term and three long-term financial goals that reflect your values, priorities, and current financial situation.

Short-Term Financial Goals (Within the Next 12 Months)

1. **Goal 1**:
   - **Specific**: What exactly do you want to accomplish?
   - **Measurable**: How will you measure success?
   - **Achievable**: Is this goal realistic given your current financial situation?
   - **Relevant**: How does this goal align with your overall financial plan?
   - **Time-bound**: When do you want to achieve this goal?
2. **Goal 2**:
   - **Specific**:
   - **Measurable**:
   - **Achievable**:
   - **Relevant**:
   - **Time-bound**:
3. **Goal 3**:
   - **Specific**:
   - **Measurable**:
   - **Achievable**:
   - **Relevant**:
   - **Time-bound**:

Long-Term Financial Goals (More Than 1 Year Out)

1. **Goal 1**:
    ◦ **Specific**:
    ◦ **Measurable**:
    ◦ **Achievable**:
    ◦ **Relevant**:
    ◦ **Time-bound**:
2. **Goal 2**:
    ◦ **Specific**:
    ◦ **Measurable**:
    ◦ **Achievable**:
    ◦ **Relevant**:
    ◦ **Time-bound**:
3. **Goal 3**:
    ◦ **Specific**:
    ◦ **Measurable**:
    ◦ **Achievable**:
    ◦ **Relevant**:
    ◦ **Time-bound**:

Once you've written your goals, keep them somewhere visible so you can refer back to them often. Whether you achieve these goals sooner or later, the process of setting them will help you stay focused, motivated, and clear on your financial path.

Conclusion

Day 2 is all about gaining clarity, which is essential for building a strong financial future. By assessing your current financial situation and setting clear, actionable short-term and long-term goals, you're laying the groundwork for success. Remember, the goals you set today will guide your decisions tomorrow—and every small step you take brings you closer to the financial freedom you deserve.

Chapter 3: Day 3 – Slashing Holiday Debt

Debt is a reality that many people face during the holiday season. The pressure to spend on gifts, decorations, and travel can lead to overspending, and before you know it, you're relying on credit cards or even taking out high-interest loans to cover the costs. While it's tempting to let holiday joy outweigh financial concerns, the consequences of accumulating debt can be severe, leaving you stressed and struggling to regain control in the new year.

In this chapter, we will focus on how to avoid falling into holiday debt traps, and if you're already carrying debt, we'll explore effective strategies for paying it off quickly. You'll learn the differences between the snowball and avalanche methods of debt repayment and create a personalized plan for eliminating your debt as part of your financial transformation journey.

Avoiding Debt Traps During the Holidays: Strategies to Avoid Credit Card Debt and High-Interest Loans

The holiday season can be a perfect storm for financial missteps. With the constant barrage of sales, promotions, and "buy now, pay later" offers, it's easy to fall into debt traps without even realizing it. But by recognizing these pitfalls and employing strategies to avoid them, you can keep your spending under control and prevent the accumulation of debt.

Common Holiday Debt Traps

1. **Credit Card Temptation**: Credit cards can be convenient, but they often come with high interest rates. If you carry a balance, that holiday gift you bought on sale could end up costing you much more in the long run due to interest charges.

2. **Buy Now, Pay Later Plans**: Many retailers offer installment payment plans that allow you to make a purchase now and pay it off over time. While these options may seem like a good deal, they can encourage overspending and come with hidden fees if you miss a payment.

3. **High-Interest Loans**: Some people turn to personal loans or payday loans to fund their holiday expenses. These loans often come with extremely high interest rates and fees, making it difficult to pay them off quickly and creating a cycle of debt.

4. **Impulse Purchases**: The holiday season is filled with sales, promotions, and marketing ploys designed to get you to spend more. If you're not careful, impulse purchases can add up, pushing you over your budget and into debt.

Strategies to Avoid Holiday Debt

1. **Set a Strict Spending Limit**: Before you start shopping, decide on a strict holiday spending limit. Use the budget you created in Day 1 to guide your purchases, and stick to it. Avoid the temptation to "just charge it" when you exceed your limit.

2. **Use Cash or Debit Cards**: One way to avoid accumulating credit card debt is to use cash or a debit card for your holiday purchases. This forces you to spend only what you have and helps you stay within your budget.

3. **Plan Your Purchases Ahead of Time**: Create a detailed list of the gifts you want to buy and set spending limits for each item. Having a plan will prevent you from making impulse purchases and keep your spending in check.

4. **Avoid Store Credit Cards**: Many retailers offer discounts or rewards for signing up for a store credit card, but these cards often come with high interest rates and fees. If you can't pay off the balance in full each month, the interest can quickly negate any savings.

5. **Focus on Meaningful Gifts, Not Expensive Ones**: It's easy to fall into the trap of thinking that more expensive gifts are better, but thoughtful, meaningful gifts are often more appreciated. Consider homemade gifts or experiences instead of pricey items.

6. **Say No to Buy Now, Pay Later**: Avoid installment payment plans unless you are confident that you can pay them off without penalties. These plans can lead to overspending and create additional financial strain after the holidays.

Debt Reduction Methods: The Snowball and Avalanche Methods Explained

If you're already carrying debt—whether from previous holidays or other expenses—it's important to develop a plan to pay it off efficiently. Two popular and effective debt repayment strategies are the **Snowball Method** and the **Avalanche Method**. Both strategies can help you reduce and eliminate debt, but they work in different ways.

The Snowball Method

The Snowball Method focuses on paying off the smallest debt balance first, regardless of the interest rate. Once you've paid off that debt, you move on to the next smallest balance, and so on. This method builds momentum and can provide a psychological boost as you quickly eliminate smaller debts.

Here's how the Snowball Method works:

1. **List your debts** from smallest balance to largest balance.
2. **Make the minimum payments** on all debts except the smallest.
3. **Allocate extra funds** to pay off the smallest debt as quickly as possible.
4. Once the smallest debt is paid off, **move to the next smallest** and repeat the process.

Example:

- Credit Card 1: $500 balance, 18% interest
- Personal Loan: $2,000 balance, 10% interest
- Credit Card 2: $3,500 balance, 20% interest

Using the Snowball Method, you would focus on paying off Credit Card 1 first, even though it has a higher interest rate than the personal loan. The idea is that paying off the smaller balance quickly provides motivation to continue paying down debt.

Pros of the Snowball Method:

- Provides quick wins that keep you motivated.
- Easy to follow and encourages discipline.
- Focuses on reducing the number of debts quickly, which simplifies your financial situation.

Cons of the Snowball Method:

- You might pay more in interest over time because you're not prioritizing high-interest debt.
- Larger debts with high interest rates could take longer to pay off.

The Avalanche Method

The Avalanche Method focuses on paying off debts with the highest interest rates first. This approach is mathematically optimal because it reduces the total amount of interest you pay over time. By focusing on high-interest debt, you'll save more money in the long run, even though it may take longer to see a debt fully paid off.

Here's how the Avalanche Method works:

1. **List your debts** from highest interest rate to lowest interest rate.
2. **Make the minimum payments** on all debts except the one with the highest interest rate.
3. **Allocate extra funds** to pay off the debt with the highest interest rate as quickly as possible.
4. Once the highest-interest debt is paid off, **move to the next highest interest rate** and repeat the process.

Example:

- Credit Card 1: $500 balance, 18% interest
- Credit Card 2: $3,500 balance, 20% interest
- Personal Loan: $2,000 balance, 10% interest

Using the Avalanche Method, you would focus on paying off Credit Card 2 first because it has the highest interest rate, even though it has a larger balance than Credit Card 1.

Pros of the Avalanche Method:

- You'll pay less in interest over time.
- It's the most financially efficient method.
- Helps you tackle the most expensive debt first.

Cons of the Avalanche Method:

- It may take longer to see significant progress, especially if your highest-interest debt has a large balance.
- Can feel discouraging if you don't see debts paid off quickly.

Choosing the Right Method for You

Both the Snowball and Avalanche methods are effective, but which one is right for you depends on your personal preferences and financial situation. If you're motivated by quick wins and like to see progress early, the Snowball Method might be a better fit. On the other hand, if you're more concerned with saving money in the long term and want to pay as little interest as possible, the Avalanche Method may be your best option.

Regardless of which method you choose, the key is to stick with it. Paying off debt requires consistency and discipline, but by using one of these structured approaches, you'll stay focused on your goal of becoming debt-free.

Action Step: Plan Your Debt Repayment Strategy for the New Year

Now that you understand the Snowball and Avalanche methods, it's time to put your plan into action. Take the following steps to create your personalized debt repayment strategy for the new year.

Step 1: List All of Your Debts

Start by making a list of all your outstanding debts, including the balance, interest rate, and minimum monthly payment for each. Use the following template:

- Debt 1: [Name of debt], [Total balance], [Interest rate], [Minimum monthly payment]
- Debt 2: [Name of debt], [Total balance], [Interest rate], [Minimum monthly payment]
- Debt 3: [Name of debt], [Total balance], [Interest rate], [Minimum monthly payment]

Step 2: Choose Your Debt Repayment Method

Decide whether the Snowball Method or the Avalanche Method is a better fit for your financial situation and personality. Write down your plan, including which debt you will tackle first and how much extra money you'll allocate toward it each month.

Step 3: Set a Debt-Free Goal

Determine when you want to be debt-free. Set a specific date or time frame for paying off each debt. This will help keep you motivated and give you a clear end point to work toward.

Step 4: Commit to Your Plan

Once you've chosen a method and mapped out your repayment plan, commit to sticking with it. Track your progress regularly, and if you receive any windfalls (like a holiday bonus or tax refund), consider putting that money toward your debt repayment to speed up the process.

Step 5: Celebrate Milestones

As you begin to pay off your debts, celebrate small victories along the way. Whether it's paying off your first credit card or eliminating a high-interest loan, these milestones are worth recognizing and will keep you motivated to continue.

Conclusion

Day 3 is all about taking control of your debt and creating a clear path to financial freedom. By avoiding holiday debt traps and implementing an effective debt repayment strategy, you'll be well on your way to eliminating your debt and reducing financial stress. Whether you choose the Snowball Method for its quick wins or the Avalanche Method for its long-term savings, what matters most is that you stay focused, disciplined, and committed to your debt repayment journey.

Slashing holiday debt is not just about getting through the season—it's about creating a debt-free future where you can enjoy holidays, and every day, without the burden of financial strain.

Chapter 4: Day 4 – A Christmas Savings Stocking: Building Your Emergency Fund

The holiday season is full of joy and excitement, but life has a way of throwing unexpected challenges at us when we least expect them. From sudden car repairs to medical bills, or even an unexpected job loss, financial emergencies can happen at any time. This is where an emergency fund comes into play—it acts as your financial safety net, helping you handle unexpected expenses without derailing your budget or falling into debt.

In this chapter, we will discuss why an emergency fund is an essential part of financial security, how to start building one, and how even small, consistent savings can lead to significant financial stability. By the end of this chapter, you'll have a clear savings plan to help you create an emergency fund that will protect you from financial disasters and give you peace of mind during the holiday season and beyond.

Why You Need an Emergency Fund: How an Emergency Fund Can Protect You from Financial Disasters

Life is full of uncertainties, and while we can't predict when an emergency will happen, we can prepare for it. An emergency fund is essentially a pool of money set aside for unforeseen circumstances that require immediate financial attention. These are not planned expenses but true emergencies that, if not covered, could lead to further financial strain.

The Role of an Emergency Fund

Having an emergency fund ensures that when a financial crisis hits, you have the resources to manage it without relying on credit cards, loans, or draining your other savings. The key benefits of having an emergency fund include:

1. **Avoiding Debt**: Without an emergency fund, most people turn to credit cards or high-interest loans to cover unexpected expenses. This leads to accumulating debt, which can be difficult to pay off, especially if the emergency is ongoing (like medical bills).
2. **Providing Financial Security**: An emergency fund gives you peace of mind, knowing that you're financially prepared for whatever life throws your way. This sense of security reduces anxiety and stress, allowing you to focus on other aspects of your life.
3. **Preventing Financial Setbacks**: Without an emergency fund, you might have to sacrifice your financial goals, like saving for retirement or a down payment on a home, to cover an unexpected expense. An emergency fund acts as a buffer, allowing you to stay on track with your long-term financial plans.

Common Emergencies That Could Require a Fund

An emergency fund is meant to cover true emergencies, such as:

- **Unexpected Medical Expenses**: Even with insurance, medical bills can add up quickly.
- **Job Loss or Reduced Income**: If you suddenly lose your job or face a reduction in income, an emergency fund can help cover your living expenses while you search for new employment.
- **Car or Home Repairs**: Whether it's a blown tire, a broken water heater, or a roof leak, these expenses can pop up at any time.
- **Family Emergencies**: Sometimes, emergencies extend beyond yourself, and you may need to help a family member in crisis.

The general rule of thumb is to have **three to six months' worth of living expenses** in your emergency fund. This should cover essential costs like rent or mortgage payments, utilities, groceries, transportation, and insurance in the event of a financial emergency.

Building a Savings Habit: Small Changes That Can Grow Into Big Savings

For many people, the idea of building an emergency fund can seem overwhelming—especially if you're living paycheck to paycheck or already dealing with debt. But the good news is that building an emergency fund doesn't require a massive lump sum to start. The key to success is consistency. By making small, manageable changes to your spending and saving habits, you can steadily build up a fund that will protect you in the future.

Step 1: Start Small, Think Big

Even if you can only afford to save a small amount each month, that's okay! It's better to start small than not to start at all. Consistency is more important than the amount you save initially. Over time, even small contributions can snowball into a substantial emergency fund. For example:

- Saving $10 a week adds up to $520 in a year.
- Saving $50 a month adds up to $600 in a year.

The key is to start, no matter how small, and keep adding to your fund regularly.

Step 2: Automate Your Savings

One of the most effective ways to build an emergency fund is to make saving automatic. Set up a direct deposit from your paycheck into a separate savings account, so the money goes into your emergency fund before you even have a chance to spend it. Automating your savings ensures that you're consistently contributing to your fund without having to think about it.

- **Set up a dedicated account**: Keep your emergency fund in a separate account from your regular checking account to avoid the temptation to spend it. Consider using a high-yield savings account so your money can grow faster with interest.
- **Automate deposits**: Schedule automatic transfers from your checking account to your emergency fund on payday or once a month. This way, you're consistently saving without any extra effort.

Step 3: Cut Back on Non-Essential Expenses

Building an emergency fund often requires making some short-term sacrifices. Look for ways to cut back on discretionary spending (things you want but don't necessarily need) and redirect that money into your savings. You don't have to make drastic lifestyle changes, but small adjustments can free up extra cash for your emergency fund:

- **Limit dining out**: Cook meals at home more often and save the money you would have spent at restaurants.
- **Cancel unused subscriptions**: Review your monthly subscriptions and cancel any that you're not using or can live without.
- **Shop smart**: Look for sales, use coupons, and avoid impulse purchases to save money on groceries and other essentials.
- **DIY Gifts and Decorations**: During the holiday season, consider making homemade gifts and decorations instead of buying expensive items.

These small changes, when made consistently, can add up to significant savings over time.

Step 4: Use Windfalls Wisely

Anytime you receive unexpected money—like a tax refund, holiday bonus, or birthday gift—consider putting a portion (or all) of it into your emergency fund. Windfalls are great opportunities to give your savings a boost without impacting your regular budget.

- **Tax refunds**: Instead of spending your entire refund, allocate a portion to your emergency fund.
- **Bonuses**: If you receive a year-end bonus or other work-related incentive, consider setting aside a percentage for savings.
- **Gifts**: Monetary gifts from family members can be a helpful addition to your emergency fund.

Action Step: Create a Savings Plan to Build an Emergency Fund

Now that you understand why an emergency fund is essential and how small changes can lead to big savings, it's time to create your personalized savings plan. This plan will help you stay on track and consistently build your emergency fund, no matter your starting point.

Step 1: Set a Savings Goal

Decide how much you want to save for your emergency fund. As mentioned earlier, a good goal is to save three to six months' worth of living expenses. To determine this amount, add up your essential monthly expenses (like rent, utilities, groceries, and transportation), then multiply by the number of months you want to cover.

For example:

- If your essential monthly expenses total $2,500, aim to save $7,500 to $15,000 for your emergency fund.
- If your expenses are $1,500 a month, your goal might be $4,500 to $9,000.

Don't be discouraged if this goal seems large—remember, you don't need to save it all at once. Start with a smaller, more manageable goal, like saving $500 or $1,000 to start, and build from there.

Step 2: Determine How Much You Can Save Each Month

Look at your budget and decide how much you can realistically save each month. If you don't already have a monthly savings habit, start with a small amount that fits your current financial situation—such as $25, $50, or $100 a month. As you make progress, you can gradually increase the amount you save.

Step 3: Automate Your Savings

Set up an automatic transfer from your checking account to your emergency fund savings account. If possible, align the transfer with your payday so you're saving consistently without having to think about it. For example:

- If you're paid bi-weekly, set up a transfer for $25 or $50 each payday.
- If you're paid monthly, schedule a transfer of $100 or more once a month.

Automating this process ensures that you prioritize savings, even when life gets busy.

Step 4: Track Your Progress

Use the provided **Emergency Fund Tracker** template to monitor your savings progress. Each time you make a deposit or reach a milestone, record it on your tracker. Seeing your emergency fund grow will motivate you to keep going, even when the goal feels far away.

Step 5: Make Adjustments as Needed

As you work on building your emergency fund, review your progress regularly. If you find that you can save more each month, increase your contributions. On the other hand, if an unexpected expense comes up, it's okay to temporarily reduce your savings until you're back on track.

Remember, building an emergency fund is a long-term goal, and consistency is more important than the speed at which you save. Even small, regular contributions will add up over time.

Conclusion

Day 4 is about taking a proactive step toward financial security by building an emergency fund. Life is unpredictable, and while we can't always control what happens, we can prepare for the unexpected. By creating a savings habit, making small adjustments to your spending, and automating your savings, you'll steadily build a financial cushion that will protect you from future emergencies.

Your emergency fund is your personal safety net—offering peace of mind and helping you avoid debt when life throws unexpected challenges your way. As you work through the next chapters, keep building your emergency fund and remember that every dollar saved is a step closer to financial freedom.

Chapter 5: Day 5 – The 5 Golden Rules of Smart Spending

We live in a consumer-driven world, where we're constantly encouraged to buy more—whether it's the latest gadget, a trendy piece of clothing, or a must-have item for the holiday season. While spending is a natural part of life, how we spend can have a profound impact on our financial well-being. Smart spending isn't about deprivation or cutting out the things you enjoy—it's about making intentional choices with your money, ensuring that every dollar works toward your goals and brings value to your life.

In this chapter, we will explore the five golden rules of smart spending, focusing on how to reassess your current spending habits and allocate your money to the things that matter most to you. By the end of this chapter, you will create a smart spending plan for the next 30 days, empowering you to take control of your finances without feeling deprived.

Reassessing Your Spending Habits: Identify Areas Where You Can Cut Back Without Feeling Deprived

The first step in mastering smart spending is taking a closer look at your current spending habits. Often, we spend money without thinking about whether the purchases are truly bringing value or joy to our lives. Over time, these unconscious spending decisions can add up and prevent us from achieving our bigger financial goals.

Step 1: Track Your Spending

To understand where your money is going, you need to track your spending. This can be done through a budgeting app, a spreadsheet, or even by reviewing your bank statements and credit card bills. The goal is to capture every expense—whether it's a morning coffee, a monthly subscription, or a trip to the grocery store.

Once you've tracked your spending for a month (or reviewed the past month's transactions), categorize your expenses into broad groups, such as:

- **Housing**: Rent or mortgage, utilities, insurance.
- **Transportation**: Gas, car payments, public transportation.
- **Food**: Groceries, dining out, coffee.
- **Entertainment**: Movies, streaming services, hobbies.
- **Shopping**: Clothing, personal care, gifts.
- **Debt Payments**: Credit cards, loans.
- **Savings**: Contributions to savings accounts or investments.

Step 2: Identify Spending Patterns

After categorizing your expenses, take a step back and look for patterns. Are there areas where you're consistently overspending? Are there categories that surprise you with how much you're spending? Common spending pitfalls often include:

- **Dining out too frequently**: Many people are surprised to find out how much they spend on dining out or takeout meals, which can easily add up over the course of a month.
- **Subscriptions and services**: Streaming services, subscription boxes, and other recurring expenses often go unnoticed because they're automatically charged to your account.
- **Impulse shopping**: Whether it's an online sale or an in-store purchase, impulse shopping can drain your budget without you realizing it.

Step 3: Cut Back Without Feeling Deprived

Smart spending isn't about cutting out all the fun or enjoyable aspects of your life. Instead, it's about identifying areas where you can cut back without feeling like you're sacrificing too much. Here are a few ideas to help you cut back in specific areas:

- **Dining Out**: If you enjoy dining out, consider reducing the frequency—perhaps limit it to once a week instead of multiple times. Cooking more at home can save a significant amount of money while still allowing for the occasional treat.
- **Subscriptions**: Evaluate all your subscriptions and cancel any that you don't use regularly or can live without. For example, if you have multiple streaming services, consider keeping only the one you use the most.
- **Shopping**: When it comes to shopping for non-essential items, implement a 48-hour rule—wait 48 hours before making a pur-

chase. This will help reduce impulse buys and give you time to consider whether you truly need the item.

By making small adjustments, you'll find that you can save money without feeling deprived or sacrificing the things you enjoy most.

The Power of Conscious Spending: How to Allocate Money to Things That Truly Matter to You

Smart spending is about more than just cutting back on unnecessary expenses—it's about being intentional with your money. This is where the concept of **conscious spending** comes into play. Conscious spending is the practice of allocating your money toward the things that truly matter to you while minimizing spending on things that don't align with your values or bring joy to your life.

Step 1: Define What Matters Most to You

Before you can allocate your money consciously, you need to understand what truly matters to you. Ask yourself:

- **What brings me the most joy or fulfillment in life?** Is it spending time with family, traveling, engaging in hobbies, or treating yourself to a nice dinner every now and then?
- **What financial goals are most important to me?** Is it saving for a home, building an emergency fund, paying off debt, or planning for retirement?

By identifying what's most important to you, you'll have a clearer sense of where you want to direct your money.

Step 2: Prioritize Spending on What Matters

Once you've identified your values and financial goals, the next step is to align your spending with these priorities. This might mean spending more in areas that bring joy or fulfillment and cutting back in areas that don't add much value to your life.

For example:

- **If family time is important**: Allocate more of your budget to experiences like family vacations or activities that you can enjoy together.
- **If financial security is a priority**: Focus on building up your savings and paying off debt, even if it means cutting back on non-essential purchases.
- **If you enjoy travel**: Rather than spending on smaller, frequent impulse purchases, direct those funds toward saving for a meaningful trip.

Step 3: Eliminate Mindless Spending

Conscious spending also involves eliminating mindless spending—the kind of spending that happens out of habit, boredom, or convenience, rather than intention. Examples of mindless spending include:

- Buying items just because they're on sale, not because you need or truly want them.
- Ordering takeout or grabbing coffee out of convenience when you could make it at home.
- Subscribing to services you rarely use.

By becoming more aware of your spending habits and focusing on aligning your purchases with your values, you'll find that your money goes further and contributes to a more fulfilling life.

Step 4: Use a Spending Framework

To practice conscious spending, consider using a simple spending framework, such as the **50/30/20 rule**:

- **50%** of your income should go toward needs (housing, utilities, food, transportation).
- **30%** should be allocated to wants (entertainment, dining out, hobbies).
- **20%** should be saved or used for debt repayment.

Adjust the percentages based on your priorities, but this framework helps ensure that you're meeting your needs, enjoying some discretionary spending, and saving for the future.

Action Step: Create a Smart Spending Plan for the Next 30 Days

Now that you've reassessed your spending habits and learned the principles of conscious spending, it's time to create a smart spending plan for the next 30 days. This plan will help you stay intentional with your money, ensuring that you're prioritizing what matters most while cutting back on non-essential expenses.

Step 1: Set a Spending Limit for Each Category

Using the spending categories you identified earlier (such as housing, transportation, food, etc.), set a spending limit for each one. Be realistic about your needs and wants, and adjust the limits based on your financial goals and values. Here's an example:

- **Housing**: $1,200
- **Transportation**: $150
- **Groceries**: $300
- **Dining Out**: $100
- **Entertainment**: $50
- **Savings**: $200

Step 2: Track Your Spending

Throughout the next 30 days, track every dollar you spend. You can use a budgeting app, a spreadsheet, or even a simple notebook to record your expenses. The key is to be consistent and honest about where your money is going.

Step 3: Make Adjustments as Needed

As you track your spending, periodically review your plan to see if you're staying within your limits. If you find that you're overspending in one category, look for areas where you can cut back. Likewise, if you're underspending in certain areas, consider redirecting that money toward savings or debt repayment.

Step 4: Reflect on Your Spending Habits

At the end of the 30 days, take some time to reflect on how your smart spending plan worked. Did you feel more in control of your money? Were there any challenges or surprises along the way? Use these reflections to adjust your plan for the next month and continue improving your spending habits.

The 5 Golden Rules of Smart Spending

To summarize, here are the five golden rules of smart spending:

1. **Know Where Your Money Is Going**: Track your spending to identify areas where you can cut back and become more aware of your financial habits.
2. **Spend with Intention**: Align your spending with your values and financial goals, prioritizing what matters most to you.
3. **Cut Back Without Feeling Deprived**: Identify areas where you can reduce spending without sacrificing the things you enjoy.
4. **Eliminate Mindless Spending**: Avoid impulse purchases and spending out of habit by practicing conscious spending.
5. **Create a Spending Plan**: Develop a spending plan for the next 30 days that aligns with your priorities and helps you stay on track with your financial goals.

Conclusion

Day 5 is about mastering the art of smart spending. By reassessing your spending habits, focusing on conscious spending, and creating a 30-day smart spending plan, you'll take control of your finances in a way that aligns with your values and goals. Remember, financial freedom isn't just about cutting costs—it's about making intentional decisions with your money that allow you to live a fulfilling life without financial stress.

Chapter 6: Day 6 – The Gift of Investment: Your First Steps Toward Wealth

For many people, investing can seem like a complex and intimidating world, but it's one of the most powerful tools for building long-term wealth. Unlike saving, which is about preserving money for short-term needs or emergencies, investing allows your money to grow and work for you over time. By learning the basics of investing and getting started with your first investment account, you can begin laying the foundation for financial security and prosperity.

In this chapter, we will explore the different types of investments—such as stocks, bonds, and index funds—and break down these concepts in a way that is easy to understand. You'll also learn how to open your first investment account and set up an automatic monthly investment plan. By the end of this chapter, you'll have taken your first steps toward growing your wealth and securing your financial future.

Understanding Investments: Stocks, Bonds, and Index Funds Explained Simply

Investing can seem overwhelming, especially with all the financial jargon that gets thrown around. But the truth is, the basic principles of investing are simpler than they seem. The key to successful investing is understanding the different types of investments, how they work, and how they fit into your overall financial plan.

What Are Stocks?

When you buy a stock, you're purchasing a small ownership stake in a company. This means you own a piece of that business, and as the company grows and becomes more profitable, the value of your shares increases. Stocks can provide high returns, but they also come with higher risk, as the value of a stock can fluctuate with market conditions.

- **How Stocks Work**: As a shareholder, you may earn money in two ways: (1) through capital appreciation, which means the value of your shares increases over time, and (2) through dividends, which are payments some companies make to their shareholders from their profits.
- **Risk vs. Reward**: Stocks tend to offer higher potential returns than other types of investments, but they also come with greater risk, as stock prices can be volatile. Over the long term, however, stocks have historically outperformed most other investments.

What Are Bonds?

A bond is essentially a loan that you make to a company, government, or other entity. When you buy a bond, you're lending money to the issuer in exchange for regular interest payments and the return of your principal (the amount you invested) when the bond matures.

- **How Bonds Work**: Bonds are considered fixed-income investments because they provide regular, predictable income in the form of interest payments. The interest rate, or "coupon," is usually fixed at the time you purchase the bond.
- **Risk vs. Reward**: Bonds are generally considered less risky than stocks because they provide steady income and are less volatile. However, they also offer lower potential returns. Bonds are a good way to balance the higher risk of stocks in your investment portfolio.

What Are Index Funds?

Index funds are a type of investment that pools money from many investors to buy a broad selection of stocks or bonds that track a specific market index, such as the S&P 500. Instead of picking individual stocks or bonds, index funds aim to replicate the performance of a specific index, which means you own a small piece of many different companies.

- **How Index Funds Work**: Index funds are passively managed, meaning they simply follow the performance of an index without frequent buying and selling of assets. This makes them low-cost and efficient.
- **Risk vs. Reward**: Index funds are generally considered less risky than individual stocks because they provide instant diversification—your money is spread across many different companies, which reduces the impact of any single company's poor performance. Over the long term, index funds have consistently pro-

vided solid returns, making them a popular choice for beginner investors.

How to Get Started: A Beginner's Guide to Opening Your First Investment Account

Now that you understand the basics of stocks, bonds, and index funds, it's time to take the next step: opening your first investment account. The good news is that getting started with investing is easier than ever, thanks to online brokerages and investment platforms that cater to beginners. Here's a step-by-step guide to help you open your first account and begin your investment journey.

Step 1: Choose the Right Type of Investment Account

There are several types of investment accounts you can open, depending on your goals. The most common types include:

1. **Brokerage Account**: A standard brokerage account allows you to buy and sell stocks, bonds, index funds, and other types of investments. You can withdraw money from the account at any time, but you'll be responsible for paying taxes on any earnings or gains.
   - **Best for**: General investing for long-term goals like buying a home or building wealth.
2. **Retirement Accounts (401(k) or IRA)**: Retirement accounts are designed to help you save for retirement, with certain tax advantages. For example, a **401(k)** is offered through your employer, while an **IRA (Individual Retirement Account)** can be opened independently. Contributions to these accounts may be tax-deductible, and earnings grow tax-deferred or tax-free, depending on the type of account.
   - **Best for**: Long-term retirement savings with tax advantages.
3. **Robo-Advisors**: If you're new to investing and don't want to manage your investments yourself, a robo-advisor can help. These

automated platforms create and manage a diversified portfolio for you based on your risk tolerance and financial goals. Popular robo-advisors include Betterment, Wealthfront, and Ellevest.

- **Best for**: Beginner investors who prefer a hands-off approach.

Step 2: Select a Brokerage or Investment Platform

Once you've decided on the type of account you want to open, you'll need to choose a brokerage or investment platform. Here are a few options to consider:

1. **Full-Service Brokerages**: These traditional firms (like Charles Schwab or Merrill Lynch) offer personalized financial advice and investment management but tend to charge higher fees.
   - **Best for**: Investors who want personalized guidance and don't mind paying higher fees for full-service management.
2. **Discount Brokerages**: Online discount brokerages (like Fidelity, Vanguard, or TD Ameritrade) offer low-cost access to a wide range of investment products. They allow you to trade stocks, bonds, and index funds with minimal fees.
   - **Best for**: DIY investors who want to manage their own investments at a lower cost.
3. **Robo-Advisors**: As mentioned earlier, robo-advisors use algorithms to automatically invest and rebalance your portfolio based on your goals and risk tolerance.
   - **Best for**: Investors who want automated, low-cost portfolio management.

Step 3: Fund Your Account

After choosing a brokerage and opening your account, the next step is to fund it. Most online brokerages and investment platforms will allow you to link your bank account and transfer money electronically. You can choose to make a one-time deposit or set up automatic contributions (more on that later).

- **Minimum Deposit**: Some platforms require a minimum deposit to get started, while others allow you to start investing with as little as $0. Be sure to check the requirements for your chosen platform.

Step 4: Decide What to Invest In

Now comes the fun part—choosing what to invest in. As a beginner, it's best to start with low-risk, diversified investments like index funds or ETFs (exchange-traded funds). These funds spread your money across a wide range of assets, reducing your risk and giving you exposure to different companies and sectors.

- **Index Funds**: As mentioned earlier, these are an excellent choice for beginners because they provide instant diversification and low fees. Look for index funds that track major indices like the S&P 500.
- **Target-Date Funds**: These funds automatically adjust their asset allocation based on your expected retirement date. They start with more aggressive investments (like stocks) and gradually shift to more conservative ones (like bonds) as you approach retirement.
- **ETFs (Exchange-Traded Funds)**: Similar to index funds, ETFs allow you to invest in a basket of assets. They are traded like stocks on an exchange, providing flexibility and liquidity.

Step 5: Start Small and Be Consistent

When you're just starting out, it's okay to start with a small amount of money. You don't need a large lump sum to begin investing. What matters most is that you start early and invest consistently over time. By making regular contributions to your investment account, you'll take advantage of **compound growth**—the process by which your money grows exponentially as your earnings are reinvested.

For example:

- If you invest $100 a month for 20 years with an average return of 7%, you'll have over $50,000 at the end of that period.
- If you invest $200 a month for the same time period, you'll have over $100,000.

The key is consistency—regularly contributing to your investment account, regardless of market fluctuations, will help you build wealth over time.

Action Step: Set Up an Automatic Monthly Investment Plan

To ensure that you're consistently investing and growing your wealth, it's important to set up an automatic monthly investment plan. Automating your investments removes the guesswork and temptation to "time the market." Instead, you'll benefit from **dollar-cost averaging**—investing the same amount regularly, regardless of market conditions.

Step 1: Determine How Much You Can Invest Monthly

Look at your budget and decide how much you can realistically invest each month. Even if you can only afford a small amount, it's better to start small and increase your contributions over time. Set a goal to invest at least 10-15% of your income if possible.

Step 2: Set Up Automatic Transfers

Most brokerages and robo-advisors allow you to set up automatic transfers from your bank account to your investment account. Decide on a specific day each month—such as the day after payday—and schedule a recurring transfer. This will ensure that you're consistently investing without having to think about it.

Step 3: Choose Your Investments

Once your account is funded, select the investments you want to purchase regularly. If you're investing in index funds or ETFs, set your account to automatically purchase shares each month when your deposit is made.

Step 4: Monitor Your Progress

While it's important to set your investments on autopilot, it's still a good idea to check in periodically. Review your portfolio at least once a year to ensure that it aligns with your financial goals and risk tolerance. If needed, make adjustments to your asset allocation or increase your monthly contributions as your financial situation improves.

Conclusion

Day 6 is about taking your first steps toward building wealth through investing. By understanding the basics of stocks, bonds, and index funds, opening your first investment account, and setting up an automatic monthly investment plan, you're creating a powerful foundation for financial growth. Remember, investing is a long-term journey—starting early, investing consistently, and staying disciplined will help you build wealth and achieve financial freedom over time.

The gift of investment is one that keeps on giving, providing you with the opportunity to grow your money and secure a prosperous future. Whether you're investing for retirement, a major life goal, or simply to build wealth, the steps you take today will have a lasting impact on your financial well-being for years to come.

Chapter 7: Day 7 – Cutting Through the Holiday Noise: How to Eliminate Financial Distractions

The holiday season can be a whirlwind of excitement, filled with festivities, family gatherings, and a constant barrage of advertisements enticing you to spend. From glittering holiday sales to limited-time offers, it's easy to get swept up in the noise and make impulse purchases that you may regret once the season is over. The pressure to spend—whether to find the perfect gift, decorate your home, or treat yourself—can be overwhelming.

In this chapter, we'll explore strategies for cutting through the holiday noise and eliminating the financial distractions that can derail your budget. You'll learn how to resist impulse buys, set clear financial boundaries, and stay focused on what truly matters during the holidays. By the end of this chapter, you'll create a personal financial boundary list to help you navigate the season without feeling pressured to overspend.

Avoiding Impulse Buys During the Holidays: Learn Strategies to Resist Sales and Marketing Ploys

The holiday season is a prime time for retailers to ramp up their marketing efforts, creating a sense of urgency with phrases like "limited-time offer" or "flash sale." These marketing tactics are designed to make you feel like you're getting an incredible deal that will soon disappear. As a result, you may feel pressured to buy items you didn't plan to purchase or spend more than you intended.

But with the right strategies, you can resist these marketing ploys and avoid impulse buys that can derail your holiday budget.

Step 1: Understand How Marketing Tactics Work

Retailers use a variety of psychological tactics to encourage impulse buying during the holidays. Some of the most common techniques include:

- **Scarcity**: Retailers create a sense of urgency by suggesting that items are in limited supply or that sales will end soon. This "fear of missing out" (FOMO) can lead you to make a purchase without fully considering whether you need the item.
- **Discount Hype**: Promotions like "50% off" or "buy one, get one free" are designed to make you feel like you're getting a bargain, even if you're not.
- **Emotional Appeal**: Many holiday ads tap into your emotions, using themes of joy, family, and togetherness to make you feel that buying their product will enhance your holiday experience.

Once you understand how these tactics work, you can be more mindful of your spending and less susceptible to their influence.

Step 2: Implement the 48-Hour Rule

One of the most effective ways to avoid impulse purchases is to implement the **48-hour rule**. When you feel tempted to make a purchase, wait 48 hours before buying the item. This gives you time to reflect on whether you really need or want it. Often, the initial excitement fades, and you may realize that the purchase isn't necessary.

- **How it works**: When you see something you want to buy, write it down or bookmark the webpage. Then, set a reminder for 48 hours later. If, after the waiting period, you still feel strongly about the purchase and it aligns with your financial goals, go ahead and buy it. But if the urge has passed, you'll know it was likely an impulse buy.

Step 3: Set a Holiday Spending Limit for Each Category

Creating a holiday budget is a crucial step in avoiding impulse buys. By setting spending limits for each category—such as gifts, decorations, and entertainment—you'll have clear guidelines to follow. This will help you resist the temptation to overspend, even when sales are enticing.

For example:

- **Gifts**: $300
- **Decorations**: $50
- **Entertainment/Activities**: $100

When you have a set budget, you can shop with intention and avoid impulse purchases that don't fit within your financial plan.

Step 4: Unsubscribe from Promotional Emails

One of the biggest sources of temptation during the holidays is your inbox, which is likely flooded with promotional emails from retailers offering holiday discounts, flash sales, and special deals. To avoid being lured into impulse buys, take a few minutes to **unsubscribe** from email lists that encourage you to spend unnecessarily. You can always re-subscribe later if you wish, but removing these distractions during the holiday season can significantly reduce the temptation to make impulse purchases.

Step 5: Shop with a List (and Stick to It)

Before you start your holiday shopping, create a detailed list of the items you need to buy—whether for gifts, holiday meals, or decorations. A shopping list acts as a roadmap, helping you stay focused and avoid unnecessary purchases.

- **How it helps**: When you shop without a plan, you're more likely to be influenced by holiday sales and marketing, leading to impulse buys. By sticking to a list, you can stay focused on your priorities and avoid veering off course.

Creating Financial Boundaries: How to Say No Without Feeling Guilty

One of the biggest challenges during the holidays is learning how to say no—both to yourself and to others. The pressure to spend can come from all directions, whether it's a friend suggesting a shopping spree, a family member encouraging you to join in on expensive holiday traditions, or even your own desire to make the season special. However, creating and enforcing financial boundaries is essential for staying on track with your budget and avoiding post-holiday regret.

Step 1: Define Your Financial Boundaries

Financial boundaries are the limits you set to protect your financial well-being. These boundaries help you stay focused on your goals and avoid overspending, especially during the holiday season. Some common examples of financial boundaries include:

- **Limiting holiday spending**: Setting a firm budget for how much you'll spend on gifts, outings, and decorations.
- **Saying no to unnecessary expenses**: Politely declining invitations or activities that don't fit within your budget.
- **Avoiding credit card debt**: Committing to paying for holiday expenses in cash or using a debit card to avoid racking up credit card debt.

Step 2: Practice Saying "No" Politely

Saying no can be difficult, especially during the holidays when you want to make others happy. However, learning to say no without feeling guilty is a crucial part of maintaining your financial boundaries. Here are a few ways to say no gracefully:

- **Be Honest**: If someone invites you to an expensive holiday outing that you can't afford, be upfront about your financial priorities. For example, you can say, "I'm focused on staying within my budget this year, so I'll have to pass on this one."
- **Offer an Alternative**: If you don't want to attend a pricey event, suggest a more budget-friendly alternative. For example, if a friend invites you to an expensive dinner, suggest meeting for coffee or a holiday walk instead.
- **Don't Over-Explain**: You don't owe anyone a detailed explanation of your financial situation. A simple "I'm prioritizing my budget this season" is enough.

Step 3: Avoid Comparison Spending

One of the biggest financial traps during the holidays is comparison spending—when you feel pressured to spend because others around you are buying expensive gifts, throwing lavish parties, or participating in costly activities. Social media can amplify this pressure, as it often showcases only the most extravagant holiday experiences.

To avoid falling into the comparison trap:

- **Focus on Your Own Priorities**: Remind yourself that your financial goals are unique to you. What others spend on the holidays shouldn't dictate how you spend your money.
- **Practice Gratitude**: Shift your mindset by focusing on the things you're grateful for, rather than what you think you're miss-

ing out on. Gratitude can help you resist the urge to overspend on things that don't truly matter.

- **Limit Social Media Exposure**: If you find that social media is contributing to feelings of comparison, consider taking a break during the holiday season or unfollowing accounts that make you feel pressured to spend more.

Action Step: Write a Financial Boundary List for the Holiday Season

Now that you understand the importance of financial boundaries, it's time to create your own boundary list for the holiday season. This list will serve as your guide, helping you stay true to your financial goals and avoid distractions.

Step 1: Identify Your Top Financial Priorities

Start by identifying your top financial priorities for the holiday season. These might include:

- Staying within your budget.
- Avoiding credit card debt.
- Saving for a specific goal (like a vacation or home purchase).
- Prioritizing experiences over material items.

Write down your top three financial priorities.

Step 2: Define Your Financial Boundaries

Next, create a list of specific financial boundaries that align with your priorities. For example:

- "I will limit my gift spending to $300 and avoid buying unnecessary items."
- "I will say no to holiday outings or events that don't fit within my budget."
- "I will avoid using credit cards for holiday purchases and stick to cash or debit."

Write down at least three financial boundaries for the holiday season.

Step 3: Commit to Enforcing Your Boundaries

Once you've defined your boundaries, commit to enforcing them. This may involve having conversations with friends and family about your budget, or reminding yourself of your priorities when faced with temptations to overspend. The more confident you are in your boundaries, the easier it will be to stick to them.

Conclusion

Day 7 is about cutting through the holiday noise and eliminating the financial distractions that can lead to overspending and impulse buying. By learning strategies to resist sales and marketing ploys, setting clear financial boundaries, and saying no without guilt, you'll be able to stay focused on your financial goals throughout the holiday season.

Remember, the holidays are about more than just spending—they're about creating meaningful memories with loved ones and focusing on what truly matters. By establishing financial boundaries and practicing smart spending, you'll enjoy a holiday season that is joyful, stress-free, and aligned with your long-term financial well-being.

Chapter 8: Day 8 – The Power of Passive Income: Earning While You Sleep

Imagine waking up in the morning to find that you've made money while you were asleep. This is the power of **passive income**—income that requires little to no ongoing effort to maintain once it's set up. Building passive income streams is one of the most effective ways to achieve financial independence, as it allows you to generate wealth without constantly trading your time for money. Whether it's earning rental income from real estate, dividends from investments, or profits from an online business, passive income can free you from the constraints of a traditional job and create financial security for the future.

In this chapter, we'll explore various passive income streams, explain how to choose the right ones based on your interests and skills, and help you develop a plan to get started. By the end of this chapter, you'll be ready to select a passive income strategy and take your first steps toward earning money while you sleep.

Exploring Passive Income Streams: Different Ways to Generate Passive Income, from Real Estate to Online Businesses

Passive income comes in many forms, and the best strategy for you will depend on your financial situation, interests, skills, and the amount of time or capital you're willing to invest upfront. Below are some of the most common types of passive income streams, each with its own advantages and considerations.

1. Real Estate Investments

Real estate is one of the most popular forms of passive income because it has the potential to generate consistent cash flow and appreciates in value over time. There are several ways to earn passive income through real estate:

- **Rental Properties**: Purchasing a rental property and leasing it to tenants can provide a steady stream of monthly income. Once the property is rented, it requires minimal effort to maintain, especially if you hire a property manager.
- **Real Estate Investment Trusts (REITs)**: If you don't want to manage a property yourself, you can invest in REITs, which allow you to buy shares in real estate companies that own and operate income-generating properties. REITs pay dividends to investors, making them a low-effort way to gain exposure to real estate.
- **Vacation Rentals**: Platforms like Airbnb or VRBO allow you to rent out a property (or even a room in your home) on a short-term basis. While vacation rentals may require more hands-on management, they can generate higher income during peak seasons.

Pros:

- Potential for steady cash flow and long-term appreciation.
- Tax advantages such as depreciation deductions.
- Diversifies your investment portfolio.

Cons:

- Requires upfront capital to purchase property.
- Ongoing maintenance and potential tenant issues.
- Property values and rental demand can fluctuate.

2. Dividend Stocks and Bonds

Investing in dividend-paying stocks or bonds is another simple way to generate passive income. Dividends are regular payments made by companies to shareholders, typically on a quarterly basis. Bonds, on the other hand, pay interest to bondholders on a set schedule.

- **Dividend Stocks**: Some companies distribute a portion of their profits to shareholders in the form of dividends. By investing in dividend-paying stocks, you can earn passive income while also benefiting from potential stock price appreciation.
- **Bonds**: When you buy a bond, you're lending money to a government or corporation, and in return, you receive regular interest payments until the bond matures.

Pros:

- Reliable source of income, especially with high-dividend stocks or bonds.
- Requires little effort once the investment is made.
- Diversifies your investment portfolio.

Cons:

- Dividends can be reduced or eliminated by companies during economic downturns.
- Stocks can fluctuate in value, leading to potential capital losses.
- Bonds offer lower returns than stocks, especially in a low-interest-rate environment.

3. Peer-to-Peer Lending

Peer-to-peer (P2P) lending allows you to earn interest by lending money to individuals or small businesses through online platforms such as LendingClub or Prosper. As a lender, you'll receive monthly interest payments on the loans you fund.

Pros:

- Higher potential returns compared to traditional savings accounts.
- Diversifies your income sources.
- You can choose the level of risk by selecting which borrowers to lend to.

Cons:

- Risk of borrower default, which could lead to loss of capital.
- Income is subject to taxes, which can reduce your overall return.
- Loans are illiquid, meaning you can't easily withdraw your money before the loan term ends.

4. Online Businesses and E-commerce

The digital age has opened up countless opportunities to earn passive income online. Whether through selling digital products, affiliate marketing, or creating an online course, online businesses can generate consistent revenue with minimal ongoing effort.

- **Affiliate Marketing**: By promoting products or services on your blog, website, or social media, you can earn commissions on sales made through your referral links. Once your content is created and ranked in search engines, it can generate passive income for years.
- **E-books and Digital Products**: If you have expertise in a particular area, you can write an e-book or create digital products (like printables or templates) that can be sold on platforms like Amazon or Etsy.
- **Online Courses**: Platforms like Udemy and Teachable allow you to create and sell online courses on a wide range of topics. Once your course is live, it can generate passive income with little ongoing effort, aside from occasional updates.

Pros:

- Low startup costs, especially for digital products and affiliate marketing.
- Scalability, allowing you to reach a global audience.
- Potential for high profit margins with minimal overhead.

Cons:

- Requires time and effort upfront to create content or products.
- Income may be inconsistent, especially in the beginning.

- High competition in the online space.

5. Royalties from Creative Works

If you're a creative person, you can earn passive income through royalties. This applies to authors, musicians, photographers, and even designers who create intellectual property that can be sold repeatedly.

- **Book Royalties**: If you write a book and publish it traditionally or through a platform like Amazon Kindle Direct Publishing (KDP), you'll earn royalties on each sale.
- **Music Royalties**: Musicians can earn royalties each time their music is streamed, downloaded, or licensed for use in commercials, movies, or TV shows.
- **Stock Photography**: Photographers can upload their photos to stock photography sites (like Shutterstock or Adobe Stock), earning royalties each time their images are downloaded.

Pros:

- Passive income for years after the creative work is completed.
- Allows you to monetize your passion and creativity.
- Scalable, with the potential to earn income from global audiences.

Cons:

- Requires significant time and effort upfront to create the work.
- Income can be unpredictable, especially in the beginning.
- High competition in creative industries.

Building a Passive Income Plan: How to Choose the Right Source of Passive Income Based on Your Interests and Skills

The key to building a successful passive income stream is to choose an opportunity that aligns with your interests, skills, and resources. Here's a step-by-step guide to help you select the right passive income stream for you:

Step 1: Assess Your Interests and Skills

Start by considering your existing skills, hobbies, and interests. Building a passive income stream requires an initial investment of time, effort, or money, so it's important to choose something that you'll enjoy working on.

- **Do you enjoy writing?** You might consider writing an e-book, starting a blog, or creating digital content for affiliate marketing.
- **Are you creative?** If so, creating an online course, selling digital products, or licensing your creative work for royalties might be a good fit.
- **Do you have capital to invest?** If you have money to invest up-front, real estate or dividend stocks might be a better option for generating passive income.

Step 2: Determine Your Available Resources

Next, evaluate your resources. Some passive income streams require significant upfront investment, while others require only time and effort. Consider:

- **Time**: How much time can you realistically dedicate to building a passive income stream? If your time is limited, consider options that require less ongoing effort, such as dividend stocks or REITs.
- **Capital**: Do you have money available to invest? If you have capital, investing in real estate or peer-to-peer lending could provide a steady stream of income. If not, you may want to focus on low-cost options like affiliate marketing or creating digital products.

Step 3: Assess Risk Tolerance

Different passive income streams come with different levels of risk. Some, like dividend stocks and bonds, offer relatively low risk with consistent returns, while others, like real estate or online businesses, carry higher risks but also higher potential rewards. Consider your risk tolerance when selecting a strategy:

- **Low-risk options**: Bonds, high-dividend stocks, and REITs.
- **Medium-risk options**: Peer-to-peer lending, rental properties.
- **Higher-risk options**: Starting an online business, investing in individual stocks, or vacation rentals.

Step 4: Set Realistic Expectations

It's important to remember that passive income doesn't happen overnight. Building a successful income stream takes time, effort, and sometimes capital. Start with realistic expectations:

- **Initial effort**: Many passive income strategies require an upfront investment of time or money to get started. For example, creating an online course or writing an e-book may take weeks or months to complete.
- **Long-term consistency**: Once your passive income stream is established, it requires less effort, but it's important to monitor and optimize it over time to ensure it continues to generate income.

Action Step: Brainstorm and Select One Passive Income Strategy to Start Working on in the New Year

Now that you've explored different passive income streams and considered how they align with your skills and interests, it's time to take action. Use the following steps to brainstorm and select one passive income strategy to start working on in the new year.

Step 1: Brainstorm Passive Income Ideas

Take a few minutes to brainstorm potential passive income strategies that interest you. Write down at least three ideas, considering factors like your skills, available resources, and risk tolerance. For example:

- "Start investing in dividend-paying stocks."
- "Create and sell an online course about digital marketing."
- "Rent out a property on Airbnb."

Step 2: Evaluate Each Idea

Once you have a few ideas, evaluate each one based on the following criteria:

- **Interest**: How passionate are you about this idea? Will you enjoy working on it?
- **Time Commitment**: How much time will it take to get started? Can you realistically commit that time?
- **Capital Required**: Do you have the financial resources to invest in this idea upfront?
- **Risk**: What is the level of risk involved, and are you comfortable with that risk?

Step 3: Choose One Strategy to Focus On

After evaluating your ideas, choose the one passive income strategy that best aligns with your goals, resources, and interests. Commit to focusing on this strategy for the next few months and create a plan for how you'll get started.

Step 4: Create a Plan for the New Year

Once you've selected your passive income strategy, create a plan to start working on it in the new year. Break down the process into manageable steps. For example, if you're starting an online business, your plan might include:

- Researching your market and target audience.
- Creating your digital product or service.
- Setting up a website and marketing strategy.

Set specific deadlines for each step to keep yourself accountable and on track.

Conclusion

Day 8 is all about unlocking the power of passive income and setting the foundation for long-term financial freedom. By exploring different passive income streams, selecting one that aligns with your interests and resources, and creating a plan to get started, you'll take a significant step toward building wealth and achieving financial independence.

Remember, passive income doesn't require constant effort, but it does require an initial investment of time, energy, or capital. By starting now and staying consistent, you can create a passive income stream that grows over time, providing you with financial security and the freedom to live life on your terms.

Chapter 9: Day 9 – The Christmas Credit Clean-Up: Repairing Your Credit Score

Your credit score is a powerful financial tool, and its importance can't be overstated. A good credit score opens doors to favorable loan terms, lower interest rates, better insurance premiums, and even increased employment opportunities. Conversely, a low credit score can make it difficult to qualify for a mortgage, car loan, or even a rental apartment. Since the holiday season is a time when many people accumulate debt, it's the perfect moment to pause and take control of your credit health.

In this chapter, we'll break down what affects your credit score, explain why maintaining good credit is essential, and offer practical tips to repair or improve your credit before the new year. By the end, you'll have a solid plan for boosting your credit score and maintaining it over time.

Understanding Credit Scores: What Affects Your Credit Score and Why It's Important

Your credit score is essentially a financial report card, measuring how responsible you are with debt. Credit scores generally range from 300 to 850, with higher scores indicating better creditworthiness. Lenders, landlords, insurers, and even potential employers may check your credit score to assess whether you're a good financial risk. That's why maintaining a healthy credit score is essential for long-term financial success.

The Five Key Factors That Affect Your Credit Score

Your credit score is calculated based on five main factors, each with its own level of importance:

1. **Payment History (35%)**: This is the most critical factor in your credit score. Lenders want to know if you've paid your bills on time in the past. Late payments, missed payments, or accounts that have gone into collections can significantly lower your score.
2. **Credit Utilization (30%)**: This refers to how much of your available credit you're using. It's calculated by dividing your total credit card balances by your total credit limits. For example, if you have a $5,000 credit limit and you're carrying a $2,000 balance, your credit utilization is 40%. Lenders prefer to see a utilization rate of 30% or less, as higher utilization indicates financial strain.
3. **Length of Credit History (15%)**: The longer your credit history, the better. This factor looks at how long your credit accounts have been open, with a longer track record of responsible credit use benefiting your score. Closing old accounts can hurt this factor.
4. **Credit Mix (10%)**: Lenders like to see that you can manage different types of credit responsibly, such as a mix of credit cards, installment loans (like a car loan or mortgage), and retail accounts.

5. **New Credit (10%)**: Opening too many new accounts in a short period can negatively affect your credit score. Each time you apply for credit, a hard inquiry is placed on your credit report, which can temporarily lower your score.

Why Your Credit Score Matters

Your credit score impacts almost every aspect of your financial life. Here's why maintaining a good score is so important:

- **Lower Interest Rates**: A higher credit score can qualify you for lower interest rates on loans and credit cards, which saves you money in the long run.
- **Better Loan Terms**: Lenders are more likely to approve you for larger loans (such as mortgages or car loans) if you have a high credit score.
- **Rental Approval**: Many landlords check your credit score as part of the rental application process. A poor score could make it harder to secure a rental apartment.
- **Job Opportunities**: Some employers, particularly in finance, may check your credit score as part of their hiring process. A low score might be seen as a sign of financial irresponsibility.
- **Insurance Premiums**: Insurers often check credit scores to determine the risk of insuring you. A low credit score can lead to higher premiums for auto or home insurance.

Now that you understand what affects your credit score and why it's essential, let's dive into actionable steps to improve it.

Improving Your Credit Score: Quick Tips for Boosting Your Score Before the New Year

Improving your credit score doesn't happen overnight, but there are several strategies you can implement to start seeing positive changes quickly. By addressing the key factors that influence your score, you can repair damage and begin building a healthier credit profile.

1. Pay Your Bills on Time

Since payment history makes up 35% of your credit score, the most effective way to improve your score is to make all of your payments on time, every time. Even one missed payment can drop your score significantly, so it's crucial to stay on top of your due dates.

- **Actionable Tip**: Set up automatic payments for recurring bills (like credit cards, utilities, and loans) to ensure you never miss a due date. If automatic payments aren't possible, set reminders on your phone or calendar a few days before the due date to give yourself time to pay.

2. Reduce Your Credit Utilization Ratio

As mentioned earlier, your credit utilization rate should ideally be below 30%. If you're carrying high credit card balances, paying them down will have a quick and positive impact on your score.

- **Actionable Tip**: Focus on paying off as much of your credit card debt as possible. If you can't pay off the entire balance, aim to get your credit utilization below 30% of your credit limit. For example, if your limit is $5,000, try to keep your balance under $1,500.

3. Don't Close Old Accounts

The length of your credit history accounts for 15% of your score. Closing old credit card accounts, even if you're not using them, can reduce the average age of your accounts and negatively affect your score.

- **Actionable Tip**: Keep old accounts open, even if you no longer use them frequently. If you have credit cards with no annual fee, consider using them for small purchases occasionally to keep the accounts active.

4. Avoid Opening New Credit Accounts

Each time you apply for new credit, a hard inquiry is placed on your credit report, which can temporarily lower your score. Applying for multiple credit accounts in a short time period can signal financial instability to lenders.

- **Actionable Tip**: Avoid opening new credit accounts unless absolutely necessary. If you're shopping for a car loan or mortgage, try to keep your credit inquiries within a 14-day window—credit scoring models typically treat multiple inquiries for the same type of loan as a single inquiry if made within this period.

5. Correct Credit Report Errors

Sometimes, mistakes on your credit report can lower your score. These errors might include incorrect information, accounts that don't belong to you, or old accounts that should have been removed. It's important to review your credit report regularly and dispute any inaccuracies.

- **Actionable Tip**: Request a free copy of your credit report from each of the three major credit bureaus (Equifax, Experian, and TransUnion) at **AnnualCreditReport.com**. Carefully review your report for any errors, such as incorrect account information, missed payments you didn't make, or fraudulent accounts. If you find errors, file a dispute with the credit bureau to have them corrected.

6. Pay Off Collections Accounts

If you have accounts that have been sent to collections, paying them off can improve your score. While the collection will still appear on your credit report for up to seven years, a paid collection is better than an unpaid one.

- **Actionable Tip**: Contact the collection agency to negotiate a payment plan or settlement. In some cases, you may be able to negotiate for the collection account to be removed from your credit report in exchange for full payment.

7. Become an Authorized User

If you have a family member or friend with a high credit score, ask if they're willing to add you as an authorized user on one of their credit cards. Being added as an authorized user allows their positive credit history to appear on your credit report, which can help boost your score.

- **Actionable Tip**: Ensure that the primary account holder has a history of on-time payments and low credit utilization. Being added to an account with a poor payment history could actually harm your credit score.

Action Step: Create a Credit Improvement Plan and Monitor Your Credit Regularly

Now that you've learned strategies for improving your credit score, it's time to put those steps into action by creating a personalized credit improvement plan. Follow these steps to get started:

Step 1: Review Your Current Credit Report

Begin by pulling your credit report from the three major credit bureaus (Equifax, Experian, and TransUnion) through **AnnualCreditReport.com**. Review each report for accuracy and identify areas where you need to improve, such as high credit card balances, late payments, or accounts in collections.

Step 2: Prioritize Areas for Improvement

Next, prioritize which areas of your credit need the most attention. If you have high credit card balances, focus on paying them down. If you have late payments or accounts in collections, work on resolving those issues. Create a list of specific actions you'll take, such as:

- Paying down credit card balances to reduce credit utilization.
- Setting up automatic payments to ensure you never miss a due date.
- Contacting collection agencies to settle or negotiate payment.

Step 3: Set SMART Credit Goals

Use the **SMART** goal-setting framework to create specific, measurable, achievable, relevant, and time-bound goals for your credit improvement plan. For example:

- **Specific**: "I will reduce my credit card balances by $1,500."
- **Measurable**: "I will pay an extra $100 each month toward my credit card balance."
- **Achievable**: "I will cut back on dining out and use that money to pay down debt."
- **Relevant**: "Improving my credit will help me qualify for a lower interest rate on a mortgage."
- **Time-bound**: "I will pay down $1,500 in credit card debt within the next 15 months."

Step 4: Monitor Your Credit Regularly

Monitoring your credit score regularly is crucial for tracking your progress and ensuring there are no errors or fraudulent activities affecting your score. Many online tools, such as **Credit Karma** or **Experian**, offer free credit monitoring services that provide real-time updates on your score and alert you to any changes.

- **Set Reminders**: Check your credit score monthly and your full credit report at least once a year. Make sure to compare your progress and adjust your plan as needed.
- **Track Your Progress**: Keep a record of your progress as you work through your credit improvement plan. This will help you stay motivated and allow you to celebrate milestones, such as paying off a credit card or resolving a collection account.

Conclusion

Day 9 is about taking control of your credit score and making it work for you. By understanding what factors influence your score and implementing practical strategies to repair or improve it, you can boost your credit before the new year and set yourself up for financial success in the future.

A healthy credit score is a critical component of your overall financial well-being. Whether you're planning to buy a home, take out a loan, or simply want to enjoy the benefits of lower interest rates, a higher credit score will open doors to better financial opportunities. With your personalized credit improvement plan in place, you're well on your way to repairing your credit and building a strong financial future.

Chapter 10: Day 10 – Maximizing the Magic of Tax Benefits

As the year comes to a close, the holiday season isn't the only thing you should be thinking about—this is also the perfect time to focus on year-end tax planning. Many people leave their tax planning to the last minute, but by taking action now, you can maximize the deductions, credits, and other tax benefits available to you, ultimately reducing your taxable income and potentially saving thousands of dollars.

In this chapter, we'll explore key tax-saving strategies you can implement before the year ends and offer tips for planning ahead to minimize your tax liability in the upcoming year. By being proactive with your tax planning, you'll be better positioned to take advantage of every available benefit and ensure that you're not leaving money on the table.

Year-End Tax Tips: How to Take Advantage of Deductions, Credits, and Other Benefits Before the Year Ends

There are several strategies you can use to reduce your taxable income before the year comes to a close. These tips can help you maximize your deductions, credits, and tax-advantaged contributions, ensuring that you're well-prepared when it's time to file your taxes.

1. Maximize Retirement Contributions

Contributing to tax-advantaged retirement accounts such as a **401(k)** or **Traditional IRA** can significantly reduce your taxable income. Contributions to these accounts are tax-deductible, meaning that the amount you contribute is subtracted from your income, lowering the amount of tax you owe.

For the 2024 tax year, the contribution limits for retirement accounts are as follows:

- **401(k)**: You can contribute up to $23,000 ($30,500 if you're 50 or older) to your 401(k).
- **Traditional IRA**: You can contribute up to $6,500 ($7,500 if you're 50 or older).

- **Actionable Tip**: If you haven't maxed out your contributions for the year, consider contributing more to your retirement accounts before December 31st. If you're unable to make a large lump-sum contribution, even small additional contributions can make a difference.

2. Take Advantage of Charitable Donations

Donating to a qualified charity not only helps a cause you care about but also provides a tax deduction. If you itemize your deductions (instead of taking the standard deduction), you can deduct charitable contributions made to qualified organizations, including cash donations and donations of property or goods.

- **Actionable Tip**: Make any charitable donations by December 31st to claim them on this year's taxes. Be sure to keep receipts or written acknowledgment from the organization for any donation over $250. If you're donating physical items like clothing or household goods, take a photo of the items and keep a record of their fair market value.

3. Harvest Investment Losses

If you've experienced losses in your investment portfolio this year, you can use a strategy called **tax-loss harvesting** to offset gains and reduce your taxable income. By selling investments that have decreased in value, you can use the losses to offset gains from other investments. If your losses exceed your gains, you can also deduct up to $3,000 of those losses against your ordinary income.

- **Actionable Tip**: Review your investment portfolio and consider selling underperforming assets to take advantage of tax-loss harvesting. Consult with a financial advisor or tax professional to ensure that this strategy aligns with your overall investment plan.

4. Prepay Medical Expenses

If your unreimbursed medical expenses exceed 7.5% of your adjusted gross income (AGI), you can deduct the excess as an itemized deduction. One way to increase your medical deduction is to **prepay medical expenses** that you expect to incur early next year. For example, if you have planned medical procedures, prescription refills, or dental work, paying for them before December 31st could help you exceed the 7.5% threshold.

- **Actionable Tip**: If you have significant medical expenses and expect to itemize deductions, consider scheduling and paying for medical services before the end of the year. Keep all receipts and documentation to support your deduction.

5. Defer Income

If you're self-employed or receive a year-end bonus, you may have some control over when you receive income. By deferring income until the following year, you can reduce your taxable income for this year and potentially stay in a lower tax bracket.

- **Actionable Tip**: If possible, delay invoicing clients or ask your employer to pay your bonus in January rather than December. This strategy can be particularly helpful if you expect to be in a lower tax bracket next year.

6. Use Your Flexible Spending Account (FSA) Funds

If you have a **Flexible Spending Account (FSA)** through your employer, now is the time to check your balance and ensure you use any remaining funds. FSAs are "use-it-or-lose-it" accounts, meaning that any funds left in the account at the end of the year may be forfeited, depending on your employer's rules.

- **Actionable Tip**: Spend your FSA funds on eligible medical expenses such as prescriptions, doctor's visits, eyeglasses, or medical supplies. Some employers allow a grace period into the next year or let you roll over a small amount of funds, but check with your HR department to confirm the rules for your plan.

Planning for Next Year's Taxes: Simple Strategies to Reduce Your Taxable Income for the Following Year

While year-end tax planning is essential, it's also important to start thinking ahead to next year. By implementing a few key strategies early on, you can reduce your taxable income throughout the year and avoid the stress of last-minute tax planning.

1. Increase Retirement Contributions Early

While many people rush to maximize their retirement contributions at the end of the year, it's much easier—and less stressful—to spread those contributions throughout the year. By contributing regularly, you'll not only reduce your taxable income but also take advantage of **dollar-cost averaging**, a strategy that helps reduce the impact of market volatility.

- **Actionable Tip**: Set up automatic contributions to your 401(k), IRA, or other retirement accounts to ensure you're consistently contributing throughout the year. If you receive a raise, consider increasing the percentage of your salary that goes into your retirement plan.

2. Contribute to a Health Savings Account (HSA)

If you have a high-deductible health plan (HDHP), you're eligible to contribute to a **Health Savings Account (HSA)**. HSAs offer a triple tax advantage: contributions are tax-deductible, earnings grow tax-free, and withdrawals for qualified medical expenses are tax-free. The funds in your HSA can also roll over from year to year, making it an excellent tool for both healthcare savings and retirement planning.

For the 2024 tax year, the contribution limits for HSAs are:

- **Individual Coverage**: $4,150
- **Family Coverage**: $8,300
- **Catch-Up Contributions (Age 55 or older)**: An additional $1,000
- **Actionable Tip**: Maximize your HSA contributions to reduce your taxable income and save for future healthcare expenses. If possible, invest the funds in your HSA to allow them to grow tax-free over time.

3. Adjust Your Withholding

If you owed a large tax bill this year or received a substantial refund, it may be time to adjust your withholding for the upcoming year. Adjusting your withholding ensures that you're paying the correct amount of taxes throughout the year, avoiding both large tax bills and interest-free loans to the government (in the form of overpayment).

- **Actionable Tip**: Use the IRS's **Tax Withholding Estimator** to determine whether you need to adjust your withholding. Submit a new **W-4 form** to your employer if necessary to ensure that the correct amount of taxes is withheld from your paycheck.

4. Contribute to a Roth IRA

If you expect to be in a higher tax bracket in the future, contributing to a **Roth IRA** can be a smart tax strategy. Unlike Traditional IRAs, contributions to a Roth IRA are not tax-deductible, but the money grows tax-free, and qualified withdrawals in retirement are tax-free as well.

- **Actionable Tip**: Consider contributing to a Roth IRA if you're eligible (income limits apply). For 2024, the contribution limits are the same as for Traditional IRAs—$6,500 ($7,500 if you're 50 or older).

5. Keep Track of Business Expenses

If you're self-employed or own a small business, keeping detailed records of your business expenses throughout the year is essential for maximizing deductions. Common deductible expenses include office supplies, travel expenses, equipment purchases, and even a portion of your home if you have a home office.

- **Actionable Tip**: Use accounting software or an expense-tracking app to keep track of business expenses. Regularly update your records to ensure you're capturing every deductible expense.

6. Invest in Tax-Efficient Accounts

If you're investing outside of tax-advantaged accounts like 401(k)s and IRAs, consider using tax-efficient strategies to minimize capital gains taxes. Tax-efficient investments, such as **index funds** or **municipal bonds**, generate less taxable income compared to other investment types.

- **Actionable Tip**: When investing in taxable accounts, focus on tax-efficient investments and use tax-loss harvesting strategies (as discussed earlier) to offset gains. Consult with a financial advisor to optimize your investment strategy for tax efficiency.

Action Step: Use the Provided Tax Checklist to Prepare for Year-End Tax Planning

Now that you have a comprehensive understanding of year-end tax strategies and how to plan for the following year, it's time to take action. Below is a checklist to help you prepare for year-end tax planning and ensure that you're maximizing all available tax benefits.

Year-End Tax Planning Checklist

1. **Retirement Contributions**:
    - Contribute the maximum amount to your 401(k) or Traditional IRA.
    - Consider opening or contributing to a Roth IRA if eligible.
    - Set up automatic contributions for next year.
2. **Charitable Donations**:
    - Make any charitable contributions by December 31st.
    - Obtain receipts or written acknowledgment for donations over $250.
    - Donate physical items and keep records of fair market value.
3. **Tax-Loss Harvesting**:

- ◦ Review your investment portfolio for losses.
- ◦ Sell underperforming investments to offset capital gains.
- ◦ Consult a financial advisor for personalized advice.

4. **Medical Expenses**:
   - ◦ Prepay any planned medical expenses if you're close to meeting the 7.5% AGI threshold for deductions.
   - ◦ Keep receipts for all medical expenses to support your deduction.

5. **Income Deferral**:
   - ◦ If self-employed, delay invoicing clients until the following year.
   - ◦ If receiving a year-end bonus, request to defer payment until January.

6. **FSA Funds**:
   - ◦ Check your FSA balance and spend any remaining funds before the year ends (if applicable).

7. **HSA Contributions**:
   - ◦ Maximize contributions to your Health Savings Account (HSA) if eligible.
   - ◦ Consider investing HSA funds for long-term growth.

8. **Withholding Adjustments**:
   - ◦ Review your tax withholding and submit a new W-4 if necessary to adjust for next year.

9. **Business Expenses** (if self-employed or a small business owner):
   - ◦ Track and categorize all deductible business expenses.
   - ◦ Review potential deductions such as home office expenses, equipment purchases, and travel.

10. **Organize Your Documents**:
    - ◦ Gather receipts, statements, and other documentation needed for tax filing.
    - ◦ Keep a record of all tax-related transactions for easy access when filing.

Conclusion

Day 10 is about making the most of the tax benefits available to you before the year ends and setting yourself up for success in the upcoming tax year. By implementing the strategies in this chapter—maximizing deductions, contributing to retirement accounts, taking advantage of charitable donations, and more—you'll reduce your taxable income and keep more money in your pocket.

Remember, taxes are one of the biggest expenses many people face, so being proactive about tax planning is crucial for long-term financial health. With your tax checklist in hand and a plan for the upcoming year, you'll be well-prepared to navigate tax season with confidence and maximize the magic of tax benefits.

Chapter 11: Day 11 – Giving Back Without Going Broke

The holiday season is traditionally a time of giving, but the desire to give back can sometimes create a conflict with your financial goals. Many people feel pressure to donate large sums to charitable organizations or buy extravagant gifts, which can lead to financial stress or even debt. However, giving back doesn't have to mean going broke. When approached thoughtfully, charitable giving can enhance your financial well-being, boost your sense of purpose, and align with your financial goals.

In this chapter, we will explore the importance of charity and how it can positively impact your financial mindset. We'll also provide smart, practical strategies to give back without straining your budget. By the end, you'll be able to create a personalized giving plan that reflects your values and supports the causes you care about, all while staying financially healthy.

The Importance of Charity: How Giving Back Can Improve Your Financial Mindset

Charitable giving is about more than just supporting causes or people in need—it also has profound psychological and emotional benefits. When you give, you're not only helping others but also fostering a mindset of abundance and gratitude, which can positively affect your relationship with money.

The Emotional Benefits of Giving

1. **A Sense of Purpose**: When you contribute to causes you care about, it fosters a deeper sense of purpose. Knowing that you're making a difference, no matter the size of your contribution, can give you a feeling of empowerment and fulfillment. This sense of purpose can help shift your mindset from one of scarcity to one of abundance.

2. **Improved Mental Well-Being**: Research has shown that giving to others can trigger the release of endorphins, often referred to as the "helper's high." This can reduce stress and boost your mood, creating a positive feedback loop where you feel happier and more connected to your community.

3. **Enhanced Gratitude**: Giving can foster a deeper sense of gratitude for the resources and opportunities you already have. Gratitude is closely linked to financial contentment because it encourages you to appreciate what you have instead of constantly striving for more. When you give, you're reminded of the blessings in your own life, which can help you build healthier spending and saving habits.

4. **Increased Financial Awareness**: When you include giving in your financial planning, it can improve your overall financial awareness. Allocating a portion of your budget to charitable contributions requires you to think carefully about your financial

priorities, which often leads to more mindful spending in other areas of your life.

How Giving Enhances Financial Success

It might seem counterintuitive, but giving back can actually improve your financial health. Here's how:

- **It Builds a Mindset of Abundance**: When you give, you signal to yourself that you have enough to share, which can help shift your mindset from scarcity to abundance. This positive outlook often leads to more effective financial decision-making and greater long-term success.
- **It Strengthens Community Connections**: Supporting causes that align with your values can open doors to new opportunities, both personally and professionally. Networking with like-minded individuals and organizations can lead to partnerships, career advancements, or personal growth, all of which can enhance your financial well-being.
- **It Encourages Financial Planning**: Allocating money for charitable donations requires thoughtful financial planning. This can lead to better budgeting habits, smarter spending, and greater control over your financial future.

Smart Ways to Give: Finding Ways to Donate and Support Causes Without Straining Your Budget

Giving back is rewarding, but it's essential to do so in a way that aligns with your financial goals and doesn't leave you financially stressed. Fortunately, there are many ways to contribute to meaningful causes without straining your budget. Whether it's through time, resources, or creative financial strategies, giving can be flexible and sustainable.

1. Donate Time Instead of Money

One of the most valuable contributions you can make is your time. Volunteering your skills or energy to a cause you care about can have just as much of an impact as a financial donation, and sometimes even more. Organizations often need hands-on help with day-to-day operations, events, or community outreach, and your time can make a tangible difference.

- **How to Get Started**: Look for local nonprofits or community organizations that need volunteers. Whether it's mentoring students, helping at a food bank, or participating in a clean-up project, volunteering allows you to give back without opening your wallet.

- **Actionable Tip**: Set a goal to volunteer a certain number of hours each month. This commitment to giving your time can be just as fulfilling as monetary donations and allows you to stay connected with the causes you care about.

2. Use Skills-Based Volunteering

If you have a specific skill or expertise, consider offering it to organizations in need. Skills-based volunteering is a powerful way to give back while using your talents in a meaningful way. For example, if you're an accountant, you could help a nonprofit with financial planning or tax preparation. If you're a graphic designer, you could help create marketing materials for a local charity.

- **How to Get Started**: Reach out to organizations whose missions resonate with you and offer your skills. Many nonprofits have limited budgets and would greatly appreciate professional services at no cost.
- **Actionable Tip**: Identify 1-2 organizations you're passionate about and reach out to them with a proposal on how you can contribute your skills. This can save the organization money and provide you with a sense of fulfillment.

3. Donate Items You No Longer Need

In addition to giving time or money, you can support charities by donating gently used items that you no longer need. Many organizations accept donations of clothing, household goods, furniture, and even electronics. Donating physical items allows you to declutter your home while helping others.

- **How to Get Started**: Research local charities or shelters that accept physical donations. Many organizations, such as Goodwill, The Salvation Army, and Habitat for Humanity, have drop-off locations for donated items. Be sure to only donate items in good condition—donations should be useful to those in need.
- **Actionable Tip**: Do a seasonal declutter and donate items you haven't used in the past year. This is a simple way to contribute to charitable causes while freeing up space in your home.

4. Participate in Community-Based Giving

Community-based giving involves supporting local causes or small-scale initiatives, which can often have a more direct and immediate impact than large charitable donations. This could include participating in food drives, sponsoring a family during the holidays, or contributing to crowdfunding campaigns for individuals in need.

- **How to Get Started**: Look for opportunities to give back within your own community. Local schools, churches, or social organizations often run giving programs during the holidays that allow you to contribute at a level that works for you.
- **Actionable Tip**: Consider adopting a family for the holiday season through a local organization or contributing to a neighborhood food bank. These small acts of kindness can make a big difference for those in need.

5. Set Up a Charitable Giving Fund

If you want to give back but need to stay within a strict budget, consider setting up a **charitable giving fund** as part of your financial plan. By setting aside a small portion of your income each month, you can create a dedicated pool of money for charitable donations without straining your finances.

- **How to Get Started**: Decide how much you can comfortably contribute to your charitable fund each month. Even if it's just $20 or $50, setting this money aside regularly allows you to give consistently throughout the year. When you come across a cause or organization you'd like to support, you can donate from this fund.
- **Actionable Tip**: Automate contributions to your charitable giving fund by setting up a recurring transfer from your checking account to a separate savings account dedicated to charitable donations.

6. Use "Cause-Related" Shopping

Many companies offer programs that allow you to give back through your purchases. For example, some retailers donate a percentage of sales to charity, or they may offer "buy one, give one" programs where for every product you purchase, a similar product is donated to someone in need.

- **How to Get Started**: Shop from businesses that are committed to social causes. For example, companies like **TOMS, Warby Parker**, and **Bomba Socks** donate products to those in need when you make a purchase. Additionally, platforms like **AmazonSmile** donate a percentage of eligible purchases to the charity of your choice.
- **Actionable Tip**: Before making a purchase, check if the retailer offers a charitable giving program. This way, you can support good causes while still meeting your own needs.

Action Step: Create a Giving Plan that Aligns with Your Values and Financial Goals

Now that you've explored various ways to give back without breaking the bank, it's time to create a personalized giving plan. This plan will help you stay focused on your charitable goals while ensuring that your giving fits within your financial means.

Step 1: Define Your Values and Priorities

Start by reflecting on the causes and issues that are most important to you. What are the values you want to reflect in your giving? Consider the following questions:

- **What causes resonate with me?** (e.g., environmental protection, poverty alleviation, education, animal welfare, etc.)
- **What organizations do I trust and want to support?**
- **Do I want to focus on local or global causes?**
- **Actionable Tip**: Make a list of the top 3-5 causes or organizations that align with your values. This will guide your giving and help you stay focused on what matters most.

Step 2: Determine Your Giving Budget

Next, decide how much you can comfortably give, either in terms of money, time, or resources. Be realistic about your financial situation and set a giving budget that aligns with your overall financial goals.

- **Actionable Tip**: Set a percentage of your monthly income to allocate for charitable giving. For example, if you decide to give 2% of your income, calculate how much that is and set aside the funds in a charitable giving account.

Step 3: Choose a Giving Method

Decide how you want to give back based on the strategies outlined in this chapter. Consider a combination of financial donations, volunteering, and in-kind donations (such as gently used items).

- **Actionable Tip**: Create a giving calendar for the year, outlining how and when you'll donate to different causes. For example:
  - **January**: Donate to a food bank.
  - **March**: Volunteer at a local animal shelter.
  - **July**: Contribute to a community fundraiser or local event.

Step 4: Monitor and Adjust Your Plan

Throughout the year, monitor your giving plan and make adjustments as needed. Life circumstances and financial situations can change, so it's essential to stay flexible while remaining committed to giving back.

- **Actionable Tip**: Set a quarterly review to check in on your giving plan. Reflect on the impact you've made and whether you want to shift focus to other causes or continue supporting the same organizations.

Conclusion

Day 11 is all about giving back in a way that aligns with your values while staying true to your financial goals. Charitable giving can be a powerful tool for improving your financial mindset, fostering gratitude, and building a sense of community. By using smart, practical strategies—such as donating time, contributing items, or setting up a charitable giving fund—you can make a meaningful difference without straining your budget.

As you move forward, your personalized giving plan will help guide your contributions and ensure that your charitable efforts are aligned with both your heart and your financial well-being. Remember, giving back isn't about the amount you give—it's about the intention behind your giving and the positive impact you make on the world around you.

Chapter 12: Day 12 – Planning for a Financially Free New Year

The excitement of the holiday season eventually fades, but the financial decisions you make during this time can have long-lasting effects. As the year draws to a close, it's the perfect time to shift your focus to the future and plan for a financially free new year. Whether your goal is to eliminate debt, grow your savings, or invest for the long term, building a clear financial vision is essential for achieving lasting financial success.

In this final chapter, we'll explore how to create a detailed financial plan for the upcoming year that aligns with your personal goals, values, and dreams. We'll also cover strategies to stay on track after the holidays, using practical tools and resources to keep you accountable. By the end of this chapter, you'll be equipped to write a comprehensive financial vision and roadmap for the next 12 months, setting yourself up for financial freedom and success.

Your Financial Vision for the Next Year: How to Build a Detailed Plan to Achieve Financial Freedom

Financial freedom is the ability to live the life you desire without being constrained by financial limitations. It means having the freedom to make choices based on your goals and values rather than on the need to make ends meet. However, achieving financial freedom doesn't happen by accident—it requires intentional planning, disciplined execution, and a commitment to long-term financial health.

Step 1: Define What Financial Freedom Means to You

Financial freedom looks different for everyone. For some, it might mean retiring early or having enough savings to travel the world. For others, it could mean being debt-free, owning a home, or having the ability to work less and spend more time with family. Before you can create a financial plan, you need to clearly define what financial freedom means to you.

Ask yourself the following questions:

- **What does a financially free life look like for me?** Is it the ability to retire by a certain age? Is it about owning your home outright or being able to quit your job and start your own business?
- **What specific financial goals do I want to achieve in the next 12 months?** Consider goals like paying off debt, increasing your emergency fund, saving for a big purchase, or investing for the future.
- **What values and priorities will guide my financial decisions?** Your financial plan should reflect your personal values, whether it's security, flexibility, independence, or generosity.
- **Actionable Tip**: Write down your vision of financial freedom. Be as specific as possible. For example: "In 12 months, I want to have $5,000 in my emergency fund, pay off my credit card debt, and contribute $400 per month to my retirement account. I

want financial flexibility to support my family without relying on credit."

Step 2: Set SMART Financial Goals

Once you have a clear vision of what financial freedom looks like for you, it's time to set specific goals that will help you achieve that vision. Use the **SMART** goal-setting framework to ensure that your financial goals are clear and achievable. SMART stands for:

- **Specific**: Your goals should be well-defined and focused. Rather than saying, "I want to save more money," be specific: "I want to save $3,000 for a vacation by August."
- **Measurable**: You need a way to track your progress. This could mean setting a specific dollar amount or percentage.
- **Achievable**: Set realistic goals that are within your reach. Don't set yourself up for failure by trying to accomplish too much too quickly.
- **Relevant**: Your goals should be aligned with your long-term vision of financial freedom.
- **Time-bound**: Set a clear deadline for each goal to keep yourself accountable.

Here's an example of a SMART financial goal: "I will pay off $2,000 of credit card debt by September 30th by making an extra $250 payment every month, and I'll set up automatic payments to ensure I stay on track."

- **Actionable Tip**: Write down 3-5 SMART financial goals for the upcoming year. These goals should be specific, measurable, achievable, relevant to your financial vision, and time-bound.

Step 3: Break Down Your Goals Into Monthly Milestones

Large financial goals can feel overwhelming, but breaking them down into smaller, more manageable steps can make them easier to achieve. Once you've set your main financial goals, break them down into monthly milestones. This will help you stay focused and track your progress throughout the year.

For example, if your goal is to save $6,000 for an emergency fund in 12 months, your monthly milestone would be saving $500 each month. Similarly, if your goal is to pay off $4,800 of credit card debt in a year, your monthly milestone would be making a $400 debt payment each month.

Breaking down your goals this way helps you stay on track and adjust your plan if needed. It also gives you small wins to celebrate along the way, which keeps you motivated.

- **Actionable Tip**: Take each of your financial goals and divide them into 12 monthly milestones. Write down these milestones so you can track your progress each month.

Step 4: Create a Detailed Budget to Support Your Goals

A well-crafted budget is the backbone of any financial plan. Your budget should align with your financial goals and ensure that you're living within your means while also making progress toward saving, investing, or paying off debt.

When creating your budget:

- **Prioritize your goals**: Allocate money toward your savings, debt payments, or investment contributions first. This ensures that you're making progress on your financial goals before spending on discretionary items.
- **Track your spending**: Use budgeting tools or apps to track your spending and make sure it aligns with your budget. Look for areas where you can cut back or make adjustments if needed.
- **Build in flexibility**: Life is unpredictable, so build some flexibility into your budget for unexpected expenses or changes in income.

Your budget should be realistic and sustainable—one that you can stick to throughout the year. As you move closer to achieving your financial goals, consider rewarding yourself with small, guilt-free treats to celebrate your progress.

- **Actionable Tip**: Create a detailed monthly budget that accounts for all of your essential expenses, savings goals, debt payments, and discretionary spending. Use budgeting apps or spreadsheets to keep track of your progress.

Staying on Track After the Holidays: Tools and Resources to Help You Stick to Your Financial Goals

Once the holiday season is over, it's easy to fall back into old habits, especially when it comes to managing your money. However, staying disciplined is crucial to achieving your financial goals. By using practical tools, resources, and accountability systems, you can stay on track long after the holiday cheer fades.

1. Use Budgeting and Tracking Apps

One of the best ways to stay on top of your finances is to use budgeting apps or financial tracking tools. These apps can help you manage your budget, track your spending, and monitor your progress toward your goals. Popular apps like **Mint, YNAB (You Need A Budget)**, and **EveryDollar** allow you to categorize expenses, set savings goals, and receive real-time notifications when you're approaching your spending limits.

- **How It Helps**: Budgeting apps provide a clear, real-time picture of where your money is going, which helps you stay accountable to your budget and financial goals.
- **Actionable Tip**: Choose a budgeting app that works best for your needs and sync it with your bank accounts. Set reminders to check your budget weekly or monthly and adjust it as needed.

2. Set Up Automatic Transfers

One of the easiest ways to stick to your financial goals is to automate your savings, debt payments, or investment contributions. By setting up automatic transfers, you ensure that you're consistently making progress on your goals without having to think about it.

For example:

- **Automatic savings**: Set up a recurring transfer from your checking account to your savings account each month.
- **Debt payments**: Schedule automatic payments toward your credit cards, loans, or other debts.
- **Investment contributions**: If you're contributing to a retirement account or brokerage account, automate those contributions so that money is invested regularly.

Automation helps remove the temptation to skip a payment or spend money meant for saving.

- **Actionable Tip**: Set up automatic transfers to your savings or investment accounts and automate debt payments to ensure you're consistently working toward your financial goals.

3. Find an Accountability Partner or Group

Having someone to hold you accountable can significantly increase your chances of sticking to your financial plan. An accountability partner could be a friend, family member, or even a financial coach. You could also join a financial group or community where members support each other in achieving their financial goals.

- **How It Helps**: Regular check-ins with an accountability partner help you stay focused on your financial vision and provide motivation when you feel like giving up.
- **Actionable Tip**: Find a trusted accountability partner and schedule monthly check-ins to review your financial progress, celebrate wins, and adjust your plan if necessary.

4. Review Your Financial Goals Regularly

As you move through the year, it's essential to regularly review and adjust your financial goals. Life can change, and your goals may need to be updated to reflect new priorities, unexpected expenses, or changes in income. Schedule a quarterly review of your financial progress to ensure you're still on track.

- **How It Helps**: Regular reviews allow you to assess what's working and what needs to be adjusted. This helps you stay flexible and adaptable, ensuring that your financial plan remains relevant.
- **Actionable Tip**: Schedule a quarterly financial review on your calendar. During each review, assess your progress toward your goals, adjust your budget if necessary, and make any changes to your financial plan.

Action Step: Write a Detailed Financial Vision and Roadmap for the Next 12 Months

Now that you've explored the steps for creating a financial plan and staying on track, it's time to take action. Use the following steps to write a detailed financial vision and roadmap for the next 12 months.

Step 1: Write Your Financial Vision Statement

Begin by writing a clear and specific financial vision statement that reflects what you want to achieve in the next 12 months. Your vision should be focused on financial freedom and aligned with your personal values. For example:

- "By the end of this year, I want to be debt-free, with a fully funded emergency fund, and contribute consistently to my retirement savings. I will live within my means while enjoying financial flexibility to support my family."

Step 2: Set SMART Financial Goals

Next, write down 3-5 SMART financial goals that will help you achieve your vision. Each goal should be specific, measurable, achievable, relevant, and time-bound. For example:

- "I will pay off $5,000 in credit card debt by December 31st by making monthly payments of $417."
- "I will save $2,400 for an emergency fund by setting aside $200 per month."

Step 3: Break Down Your Goals Into Monthly Milestones

For each goal, break it down into monthly milestones to track your progress. Write down the specific actions you'll take each month to stay on track. For example:

- "In January, I will reduce my credit card balance by $417."
- "In February, I will save $200 for my emergency fund."

Step 4: Create a Detailed Budget

Write a detailed budget that supports your financial goals. Include all essential expenses (like housing, utilities, and groceries), as well as allocations for savings, debt repayment, and discretionary spending.

Step 5: Plan for Accountability

Choose an accountability partner or group and schedule regular check-ins to review your progress. Make a plan for how often you'll review your budget, track your goals, and adjust your financial plan as needed.

Conclusion

Day 12 is about laying the foundation for a financially free new year. By building a clear financial vision, setting SMART goals, creating a detailed budget, and using tools and resources to stay on track, you'll be well-prepared to achieve your financial goals and experience lasting financial success.

Remember, financial freedom is not a one-time event—it's a journey that requires planning, discipline, and regular reflection. As you move forward, your financial vision and roadmap will guide you toward the life you desire, helping you create a future filled with financial security and flexibility. With a solid plan in place, you're on the path to making this year your best financial year yet!

Appendices: Tools and Resources for Financial Transformation

Appendix A – Financial Worksheets: Printable Worksheets for Budgeting, Savings, Debt Repayment, and More

This appendix provides a comprehensive collection of worksheets designed to help you take action on the strategies and plans outlined in the previous chapters. Whether you're building a budget, tracking your savings, or managing debt repayment, these worksheets will serve as practical tools for organizing and monitoring your financial progress. You can print them out and fill them in manually or use them digitally, depending on your preference.

Each worksheet is explained in detail so you understand how to use it effectively. Let's walk through the essential financial worksheets that will support your journey toward financial freedom.

1. Monthly Budget Worksheet

A budget is the cornerstone of your financial plan. This worksheet helps you create a clear picture of your income, expenses, and savings goals for each month, allowing you to take control of your spending and ensure that your financial habits align with your long-term goals.

How to Use the Monthly Budget Worksheet:

- **Step 1**: List your total **monthly income** from all sources (e.g., salary, freelance work, side gigs).
- **Step 2**: Break down your **fixed expenses**, which are essential expenses that remain the same each month (e.g., rent, utilities, insurance, loan payments).
- **Step 3**: List your **variable expenses**, which fluctuate month to month (e.g., groceries, dining out, entertainment).
- **Step 4**: Allocate funds for your **savings goals**, such as your emergency fund, retirement contributions, or saving for a large purchase.
- **Step 5**: Track any **debt payments**, including credit card payments, loans, or other financial obligations.

- **Step 6**: Calculate the difference between your total income and your total expenses. If you have a positive balance, decide how to allocate the surplus (e.g., toward savings or debt repayment). If you have a negative balance, look for areas where you can cut back.

Monthly Budget Worksheet Template:

Income	Amount
Salary	$
Freelance/Side Hustles	$
Other Income	$
Total Monthly Income	**$**

Fixed Expenses	Amount
Rent/Mortgage	$
Utilities	$
Insurance	$
Transportation	$
Subscriptions	$
Loan Payments	$
Total Fixed Expenses	**$**

Variable Expenses	Amount
Groceries	$

Variable Expenses	Amount
Dining Out	$
Entertainment	$
Clothing	$
Miscellaneous	$
Total Variable Expenses	**$**

Savings Goals	Amount
Emergency Fund	$
Retirement Contributions	$
Vacation Fund	$
Other Savings	$
Total Savings	**$**

Debt Payments	Amount
Credit Card 1	$
Credit Card 2	$
Student Loan	$
Other Debt	$
Total Debt Payments	**$**

Summary	Amount
Total Monthly Income	$
Total Expenses (Fixed + Variable)	$
Total Savings	$
Total Debt Payments	$
Net Balance	$

2. Savings Tracker

Setting specific savings goals and tracking your progress is key to building financial security. Whether you're saving for an emergency fund, a vacation, or a down payment on a home, this worksheet will help you monitor your savings and stay motivated.

How to Use the Savings Tracker:

- **Step 1**: Identify your savings goals (e.g., emergency fund, new car, vacation).
- **Step 2**: Set a **target amount** for each goal and write it in the appropriate column.
- **Step 3**: Record your **starting balance** and track each deposit you make toward your goal.
- **Step 4**: Monitor your progress as you get closer to reaching your target.
- **Step 5**: Celebrate each milestone (e.g., when you reach 25%, 50%, 75%, and 100% of your goal).

Savings Tracker Template:

Savings Goal	Target Amount	Starting Balance	Date	Deposit	New Balance	Progress (%)
Emergency Fund	$	$		$	$	%
Vacation Fund	$	$		$	$	%
Home Down Payment	$	$		$	$	%
Other Savings Goal	$	$		$	$	%

3. Debt Repayment Plan

If you're working to pay down debt, having a clear repayment strategy is essential. This worksheet will help you organize your debts, prioritize which ones to pay off first, and track your progress as you reduce your debt over time.

How to Use the Debt Repayment Plan Worksheet:

- **Step 1**: List each of your debts, including the total balance, interest rate, and minimum monthly payment.
- **Step 2**: Choose a repayment strategy, such as the **debt snowball** (paying off the smallest balance first) or the **debt avalanche** (paying off the debt with the highest interest rate first).
- **Step 3**: Track each payment you make and adjust your strategy as you make progress.
- **Step 4**: Celebrate each milestone as you pay off your debts.

Debt Repayment Plan Template:

Debt	Balance	Interest Rate (%)	Minimum Payment	Extra Payment	Total Payment	New Balance
Credit Card 1	$	%	$	$	$	$
Credit Card 2	$	%	$	$	$	$
Student Loan	$	%	$	$	$	$
Car Loan	$	%	$	$	$	$

4. Net Worth Tracker

Your **net worth** is a measure of your overall financial health. It's calculated by subtracting your liabilities (what you owe) from your assets (what you own). This worksheet will help you calculate and track your net worth over time, allowing you to see the bigger picture of your financial progress.

How to Use the Net Worth Tracker:

- **Step 1**: List all of your assets, including cash, investments, property, and any other items of value.
- **Step 2**: List all of your liabilities, such as credit card debt, loans, and other financial obligations.
- **Step 3**: Subtract your total liabilities from your total assets to calculate your net worth.
- **Step 4**: Update this worksheet periodically (e.g., quarterly or annually) to track how your net worth changes over time.

Net Worth Tracker Template:

Assets	Value
Cash and Savings	$
Retirement Accounts	$
Investment Accounts	$
Home (Market Value)	$
Car(s) (Market Value)	$
Other Assets	$
Total Assets	**$**

Liabilities	Balance
Mortgage	$
Car Loan	$
Credit Card 1	$
Credit Card 2	$
Student Loan	$
Other Liabilities	$
Total Liabilities	$

Net Worth Calculation	Amount
Total Assets	$
Total Liabilities	$
Net Worth (Assets - Liabilities)	$

5. Financial Goal Planner

This worksheet is designed to help you set, prioritize, and track your financial goals over the next 12 months. By outlining each goal and the steps needed to achieve it, you'll stay focused and motivated as you work toward financial freedom.

How to Use the Financial Goal Planner:

- **Step 1**: Write down your financial goals for the next 12 months. Be specific about what you want to achieve.
- **Step 2**: Set a target completion date for each goal.
- **Step 3**: Break each goal down into smaller, actionable steps.
- **Step 4**: Track your progress and make adjustments as needed.

Financial Goal Planner Template:

Financial Goal	Target Date	Action Steps	Progress
Build an Emergency Fund	6/30/2024	1. Set up automatic savings transfer of $200/month	50%
Pay Off Credit Card Debt	12/31/2024	1. Pay $500/month toward credit card balance	25%
Save for a Vacation	8/31/2024	1. Save $150/month	30%

6. Annual Financial Review

At the end of the year, it's important to review your financial progress and reassess your goals for the upcoming year. This worksheet will guide you through an annual financial review, allowing you to reflect on your successes, identify areas for improvement, and set new goals for the next 12 months.

How to Use the Annual Financial Review Worksheet:

- **Step 1**: Reflect on the past year's financial successes and challenges. What went well? What could have been improved?
- **Step 2**: Review your financial goals from the previous year and note which ones you achieved.
- **Step 3**: Identify new financial goals for the upcoming year and create an action plan.

Annual Financial Review Template:

Financial Successes	Challenges
1. Paid off credit card debt by June	1. Struggled to save consistently
2. Increased retirement contributions	2. Overspent on discretionary items

Goals Achieved	New Financial Goals
1. Saved $5,000 for an emergency fund	1. Save $10,000 for a home down payment by December 2025
2. Increased credit score by 50 points	2. Increase retirement contributions to 15% of income

Conclusion

The financial worksheets in this appendix are designed to help you stay organized, track your progress, and remain focused on your financial goals. Whether you're budgeting, saving, paying off debt, or planning for the future, these tools will provide the structure and support you need to achieve financial success.

Remember, the key to financial freedom is consistency. By using these worksheets regularly and reviewing your progress, you'll gain greater control over your finances and move closer to the life of financial freedom you envision.

Appendix B – Recommended Resources: Books, Websites, and Apps for Further Financial Education

Achieving financial freedom is a continuous journey that requires knowledge, discipline, and the right tools. To support you on this path, this appendix provides a curated list of books, websites, and apps that offer further financial education and practical guidance. Whether you're looking to deepen your understanding of personal finance, improve your budgeting skills, or explore investment strategies, these resources will help you stay informed and empowered.

Each resource is categorized and includes a brief description of how it can benefit you. From classic personal finance books to cutting-edge apps that help you manage your money, this appendix offers a comprehensive guide to financial literacy tools.

1. Recommended Books

Books are an excellent way to expand your knowledge of personal finance and wealth-building strategies. Below are some of the most popular and highly recommended books in the field of financial education.

1.1. *Your Money or Your Life* by Vicki Robin and Joe Dominguez

This personal finance classic emphasizes the connection between money and life satisfaction. It walks readers through a nine-step process to transform their relationship with money, eliminate debt, and achieve financial independence.

- **Why Read It?**: This book provides a holistic approach to managing your finances and rethinking how you value time and money. It's perfect for those looking to align their spending with their personal values.

1.2. *The Total Money Makeover* by Dave Ramsey

Dave Ramsey's no-nonsense approach to personal finance has helped millions of people get out of debt and build wealth. The book focuses on creating a solid financial foundation through budgeting, saving, and investing, with a strong emphasis on becoming debt-free.

- **Why Read It?**: If you're looking for a step-by-step plan to eliminate debt, build an emergency fund, and start investing, this is a must-read. Ramsey's advice is straightforward and actionable.

1.3. *I Will Teach You to Be Rich* by Ramit Sethi

Ramit Sethi's book is geared toward millennials and young adults looking to build wealth through smart money management. The book covers topics like optimizing your credit cards, automating your finances, and investing in the stock market.

- **Why Read It?**: This book offers practical, no-frills advice on how to take control of your money, with an emphasis on automation and maximizing rewards. It's ideal for those who want a simple yet effective strategy for managing their finances.

1.4. *The Simple Path to Wealth* by JL Collins

Originally written as a series of letters to his daughter, JL Collins' book provides a straightforward guide to financial independence through investing in low-cost index funds. The book covers topics such as stock market investing, the importance of financial independence, and how to live a simple, fulfilling life.

- **Why Read It?**: This book is an excellent resource for beginners who want to learn about long-term investing, particularly in index funds. It offers a simple, easy-to-follow strategy for building wealth.

1.5. *Rich Dad Poor Dad* **by Robert T. Kiyosaki**

One of the most famous personal finance books of all time, *Rich Dad Poor Dad* explores the differences in mindset between the wealthy and the middle class. Kiyosaki uses his own experiences to illustrate the importance of financial education, investing, and building assets.

- **Why Read It?**: This book is a great introduction to the concepts of wealth-building, investing, and financial independence. It encourages readers to think differently about money and how to make it work for them.

2. Recommended Websites

Websites provide up-to-date information, tools, and educational content to help you manage your money and stay informed about personal finance trends. Below are some trusted websites that offer a wealth of resources for improving your financial literacy.

2.1. NerdWallet

NerdWallet is a comprehensive personal finance website that offers expert advice on topics such as credit cards, mortgages, investing, and banking. The site also provides tools for comparing financial products, such as credit card rewards and interest rates.

- **Why Visit?**: NerdWallet's tools and reviews make it easy to compare financial products and find the best options for your situation. It's a great resource for researching credit cards, loans, and investment accounts.

2.2. Investopedia

Investopedia is an educational website that provides a wealth of information on investing, finance, and economics. The site includes tutorials, definitions, articles, and a stock market simulator to help users understand key financial concepts.

- **Why Visit?**: Investopedia is one of the best resources for learning about investing and financial markets. Its comprehensive guides and easy-to-understand articles make complex topics accessible for beginners and advanced learners alike.

2.3. The Balance

The Balance offers clear, actionable financial advice on a wide range of topics, from budgeting and saving to investing and retirement planning. The site is designed to help individuals make informed financial decisions and improve their financial health.

- **Why Visit?**: The Balance's straightforward, easy-to-read content is perfect for those looking to improve their financial knowledge without feeling overwhelmed. It covers a variety of personal finance topics, making it an excellent all-in-one resource.

2.4. Mr. Money Mustache

Mr. Money Mustache is a popular personal finance blog that focuses on the principles of financial independence and early retirement (FIRE). The blog emphasizes frugality, investing, and living a simple, fulfilling life.

- **Why Visit?**: If you're interested in achieving financial independence and retiring early, Mr. Money Mustache offers inspiring content and practical advice on how to cut expenses and invest wisely for the long term.

2.5. Bogleheads

Bogleheads is an online community that follows the investment philosophy of Vanguard founder John C. Bogle, who advocated for low-cost index fund investing. The website features forums, investment guides, and a wiki with educational content on personal finance and investing.

- **Why Visit?**: Bogleheads is an excellent resource for those looking to adopt a passive, low-cost investment strategy. The community and resources on the site provide valuable insights for both new and experienced investors.

3. Recommended Apps

Personal finance apps make it easy to manage your money, track your spending, and stay on top of your financial goals. Here are some of the best apps for budgeting, saving, and investing.

3.1. Mint

Mint is a free budgeting app that allows you to track all of your financial accounts in one place. It automatically categorizes your transactions, helps you set financial goals, and sends alerts when you're close to overspending.

- **Why Use It?**: Mint is ideal for anyone who wants to take control of their budget and monitor their spending habits in real time. The app's user-friendly interface makes it easy to create and stick to a budget.

3.2. YNAB (You Need A Budget)

YNAB is a powerful budgeting app based on the principle of giving every dollar a job. It focuses on helping users plan their spending, build an emergency fund, and get out of debt. The app also provides educational content on budgeting and financial management.

- **Why Use It?**: YNAB is perfect for those who want a proactive approach to budgeting. Its zero-based budgeting system encourages users to plan for every dollar and stay in control of their finances.

3.3. Personal Capital

Personal Capital is both a budgeting and investment management app. It allows you to track your income, expenses, and investments in one place, offering tools for retirement planning and wealth management. The app also provides insights into your investment portfolio's performance and asset allocation.

- **Why Use It?**: Personal Capital is a great choice for individuals looking to manage both their day-to-day budget and long-term investments. It's especially useful for tracking your net worth and planning for retirement.

3.4. Acorns

Acorns is an investment app that rounds up your everyday purchases to the nearest dollar and invests the spare change in a diversified portfolio. It's designed to make investing simple and automatic for beginners.

- **Why Use It?**: Acorns is ideal for those who are new to investing and want an easy way to get started. The app's automated features make it effortless to build an investment portfolio with small, consistent contributions.

3.5. PocketGuard

PocketGuard is a budgeting app that helps you manage your money by showing how much disposable income you have after accounting for bills, savings goals, and essential expenses. It links to your bank accounts and provides real-time updates on your financial status.

- **Why Use It?**: PocketGuard is perfect for individuals who want a clear, real-time snapshot of their financial situation. Its "In My Pocket" feature shows how much money you can safely spend without compromising your financial goals.

Conclusion

This appendix provides a variety of resources that cater to different aspects of financial education, from books that inspire and educate to websites and apps that offer practical tools for managing your finances. Whether you're looking to improve your budgeting skills, learn more about investing, or take control of your debt, these resources will help guide you on your journey to financial freedom.

Remember, financial success is built on continuous learning and discipline. By using the resources in this appendix, you'll gain the knowledge, tools, and confidence to make informed decisions, grow your wealth, and achieve your long-term financial goals.

Appendix C – Holiday Financial Checklists: Handy Checklists for Controlling Spending and Staying on Track During the Holidays

The holiday season is a time of celebration, family gatherings, and gift-giving, but it can also be a time when financial discipline takes a back seat. With the excitement of holiday sales, festive events, and increased social obligations, it's easy to overspend and derail your financial goals. To help you stay on track, this appendix provides several detailed financial checklists that cover everything from holiday budgeting to gift planning and managing holiday debt.

These checklists are designed to keep you organized and mindful of your financial limits, ensuring that you enjoy the holidays without experiencing financial stress. Print them out or use them digitally to guide your holiday planning and spending.

1. Holiday Budget Checklist

The first step to controlling holiday spending is creating a detailed holiday budget. This checklist will help you outline your expected expenses, set spending limits, and prioritize your financial goals during the holiday season.

How to Use the Holiday Budget Checklist:

- **Step 1**: Determine how much you can realistically afford to spend during the holidays without going into debt.
- **Step 2**: List all the categories where you expect to spend money (e.g., gifts, food, travel, decorations).
- **Step 3**: Set a spending limit for each category and track your actual spending to ensure you stay within your budget.

Holiday Budget Checklist Template:

Category	Planned Spending	Actual Spending	Notes
Gifts	$	$	List all people to buy for
Holiday Meals/Food	$	$	Include special meals and parties
Travel	$	$	Transportation, accommodations
Decorations	$	$	Indoor and outdoor decorations
Charitable Giving	$	$	Donations to causes you support
Holiday Events/Entertainment	$	$	Concerts, parties, and activities
Miscellaneous	$	$	Unexpected or last-minute expenses

Category	Planned Spending	Actual Spending	Notes
Total Planned Spending	$		

2. Gift Planning Checklist

Gift-giving is often the largest expense during the holiday season, so it's essential to plan your gifts thoughtfully. This checklist will help you track who you're buying for, set a budget for each person, and brainstorm gift ideas that fit within your financial plan.

How to Use the Gift Planning Checklist:

- **Step 1**: List all the people you plan to buy gifts for, including family members, friends, coworkers, and any additional categories like teachers or service workers.
- **Step 2**: Set a gift budget for each person based on your overall holiday budget.
- **Step 3**: Brainstorm thoughtful and meaningful gift ideas that align with your budget, and check off each gift as it's purchased.

Gift Planning Checklist Template:

Recipient	Budget	Gift Ideas	Purchased (Yes/No)	Actual Cost
Family Member 1	$	Example: Book, candle, scarf	Yes / No	$
Family Member 2	$	Example: Kitchen gadget	Yes / No	$
Friend 1	$	Example: Coffee gift set	Yes / No	$

Recipient	Budget	Gift Ideas	Purchased (Yes/No)	Actual Cost
Coworker 1	$	Example: Desk organizer	Yes / No	$
Teacher/ Service Worker 1	$	Example: Gift card, chocolates	Yes / No	$
Miscellaneous	$		Yes / No	$
Total Gift Budget	**$**			**$**

3. Holiday Shopping Checklist

It's easy to get caught up in holiday sales and overspend on impulse purchases. This shopping checklist is designed to help you stay organized and intentional when shopping, whether online or in-store. Use it to track your planned purchases, stay within budget, and avoid unnecessary expenses.

How to Use the Holiday Shopping Checklist:

- **Step 1**: List the items you plan to purchase, whether they're gifts, decorations, or items for holiday meals and parties.
- **Step 2**: Compare prices at different retailers to find the best deals.
- **Step 3**: Check off each item as you purchase it, and track the actual cost against your planned budget.

Holiday Shopping Checklist Template:

Item	Category	Planned Cost	Retailer/Price Comparison	Purchased (Yes/No)	Actual Cost
Holiday Tree Decorations	Decorations	$	Store A: $10, Store B: $12	Yes / No	$
Turkey for Holiday Dinner	Food	$	Grocery A: $20, Grocery B: $18	Yes / No	$
Gift for Partner	Gift	$	Online Store A: $40, Store B: $45	Yes / No	$
Family Board Game	Entertainment	$	Online A: $25, Store B: $30	Yes / No	$
Gift Wrap	Miscellaneous	$	Dollar Store: $5	Yes / No	$

Item	Cate-gory	Planned Cost	Re-tailer/Price Compari-son	Pur-chased (Yes/No)	Actual Cost
Total Planned Spending	$				$

4. Holiday Travel Checklist

For many, travel is a significant expense during the holiday season. This checklist will help you plan and manage your travel costs, whether you're visiting family across the country or taking a holiday vacation. By organizing your travel plans, you can avoid last-minute price spikes and budget effectively for transportation, accommodations, and other expenses.

How to Use the Holiday Travel Checklist:

- **Step 1**: List all the travel expenses you expect to incur, such as flights, gas, or hotel accommodations.
- **Step 2**: Research and book travel early to get the best rates.
- **Step 3**: Track your actual spending against your travel budget and account for any additional travel-related expenses.

Holiday Travel Checklist Template:

Travel Expense	Planned Cost	Actual Cost	Notes
Flights	$	$	Book early for best rates
Gas for Road Trip	$	$	Calculate miles and gas prices
Hotel/Accommodation	$	$	Compare hotel rates, Airbnb
Rental Car	$	$	Optional
Parking/Transportation	$	$	Public transport, taxis, etc.
Meals While Traveling	$	$	Account for dining out
Miscellaneous Travel Costs	$	$	Travel insurance, tolls, etc.
Total Travel Budget	**$**	**$**	

5. Holiday Debt Prevention Checklist

The holidays are a time when many people rely on credit cards to cover extra expenses. This checklist will help you stay mindful of your holiday spending and avoid falling into debt traps. Use it to set limits on credit card usage, track your holiday debt, and create a plan to pay it off quickly.

How to Use the Holiday Debt Prevention Checklist:

- **Step 1**: Set a clear limit on how much you're willing to charge on your credit cards during the holiday season.
- **Step 2**: Track each purchase made with credit cards and compare it to your spending limits.
- **Step 3**: Create a post-holiday repayment plan to pay off any credit card debt as quickly as possible.

Holiday Debt Prevention Checklist Template:

Credit Card	Limit for Holiday Spending	Amount Charged	Remaining Balance	Planned Repayment
Credit Card 1	$	$	$	Pay $ per month
Credit Card 2	$	$	$	Pay $ per month
Store Credit Card	$	$	$	Pay $ per month
Total Holiday Debt	$	$	$	

6. Post-Holiday Financial Recovery Checklist

After the holidays, it's essential to review your spending, assess any debt you've incurred, and create a recovery plan to get back on track. This checklist will guide you through the steps needed to recover financially after the holidays and ensure you start the new year on solid financial footing.

How to Use the Post-Holiday Financial Recovery Checklist:

- **Step 1**: Review your holiday spending and compare it to your budget.
- **Step 2**: Assess any credit card debt or additional expenses incurred during the holidays.
- **Step 3**: Create a post-holiday financial plan, which may include adjusting your budget, cutting discretionary spending, or increasing savings contributions.

Post-Holiday Financial Recovery Checklist Template:

Task	Completion Date	Notes
Review total holiday spending		Compare actual spending to budget
Assess credit card balances		List total debt incurred
Create a debt repayment plan		Prioritize high-interest debts
Adjust budget for the new year		Reduce discretionary expenses
Rebuild emergency fund (if needed)		Replenish savings after holidays
Review savings goals for the year		Set goals for the new year
Monitor financial progress		Monthly reviews

Conclusion

These holiday financial checklists are designed to help you navigate the busy holiday season while staying on track with your financial goals. By planning ahead, setting spending limits, and being mindful of your budget, you can enjoy the holidays without the stress of financial fallout.

Use these checklists as tools to keep yourself organized and intentional with your holiday spending. Remember, financial health is about balance—celebrating the season without compromising your long-term goals is the key to financial freedom.

Appendix D – Glossary of Financial Terms: Easy-to-Understand Definitions of Key Financial Concepts

This glossary provides simple, clear definitions of the key financial terms and concepts mentioned throughout the book. Understanding these terms is crucial for managing your finances effectively, making informed decisions, and working toward financial freedom. Whether you're new to personal finance or just need a refresher, this glossary will serve as a helpful reference.

A

Account Balance

The total amount of money currently in a financial account, such as a checking, savings, or investment account. For credit cards, the account balance represents the amount owed.

Adjusted Gross Income (AGI)

Your total gross income minus specific deductions (such as student loan interest or retirement contributions). AGI is used to determine your taxable income.

Amortization

The process of gradually paying off a debt (such as a loan or mortgage) over time through regular payments. Each payment covers both the principal and interest.

Annual Percentage Rate (APR)

The yearly interest rate charged on borrowed money (such as on credit cards or loans) or earned through investments. APR includes any fees or costs associated with the transaction.

Asset

Anything of value that you own, including cash, real estate, stocks, bonds, and personal property. Assets can be used to generate income or provide financial security.

B

Balance Transfer

The process of moving debt from one credit card to another, typically to take advantage of a lower interest rate. Balance transfers can help reduce interest costs but may involve fees.

Bankruptcy

A legal process that allows individuals or businesses unable to repay debts to either eliminate the debt or repay it under the protection of a court. Filing for bankruptcy can negatively impact your credit score.

Bear Market

A period when the prices of securities (such as stocks) are falling, typically by 20% or more. Bear markets can last for months or even years and are often associated with economic downturns.

Bond

A fixed-income investment where you lend money to a government, corporation, or other entity in exchange for regular interest payments. At the end of the bond's term, the principal is returned to you.

Budget

A financial plan that outlines expected income and expenses over a specific period (such as a month or year). A budget helps manage spending, track savings, and ensure financial goals are met.

C

Capital Gain

The profit earned from the sale of an asset, such as stocks, bonds, or real estate, when the selling price exceeds the purchase price. Capital gains are subject to taxes.

Cash Flow

The movement of money in and out of your accounts. Positive cash flow means more money is coming in than going out, while negative cash flow means more money is being spent than earned.

Certificate of Deposit (CD)

A savings account that holds a fixed amount of money for a fixed period at a fixed interest rate. CDs typically offer higher interest rates than regular savings accounts but impose penalties for early withdrawal.

Compound Interest

Interest calculated not only on the initial principal but also on the accumulated interest from previous periods. Compound interest allows investments or savings to grow faster over time.

Credit Report

A detailed record of an individual's credit history, including information about loans, credit cards, payment history, and any debts in collections. Credit reports are used by lenders to assess creditworthiness.

Credit Score

A numerical representation of your creditworthiness, typically ranging from 300 to 850. It is based on your credit history and is used by lenders to determine whether to approve you for loans or credit cards, and at what interest rates.

D

Debt-to-Income Ratio (DTI)

A measure of your total monthly debt payments compared to your monthly gross income. Lenders use the DTI ratio to determine your ability to manage monthly payments and repay debts.

Deduction

An expense that can be subtracted from your gross income to reduce your taxable income. Common deductions include mortgage interest, charitable donations, and medical expenses.

Depreciation

The gradual decrease in the value of an asset over time, often due to wear and tear or obsolescence. Depreciation is used for tax purposes to account for the declining value of assets such as vehicles or equipment.

Diversification

A risk management strategy that involves spreading investments across various asset classes (e.g., stocks, bonds, real estate) to reduce the impact of poor performance by any one asset.

Dividend

A portion of a company's profits that is paid to shareholders, typically on a quarterly basis. Dividends provide investors with a regular income in addition to potential capital gains.

E

Emergency Fund

A savings account set aside to cover unexpected expenses, such as medical emergencies, car repairs, or job loss. A well-funded emergency fund typically covers three to six months of living expenses.

Equity

The value of ownership in an asset, such as real estate or a business. In the case of a home, equity is the market value of the property minus any outstanding mortgage balance.

Estate Planning

The process of preparing for the transfer of an individual's assets after death. Estate planning typically includes writing a will, setting up trusts, and choosing beneficiaries for life insurance and retirement accounts.

Exchange-Traded Fund (ETF)

A type of investment fund that holds a basket of assets, such as stocks or bonds, and is traded on an exchange like a stock. ETFs provide diversification and are often lower-cost than mutual funds.

F

Fixed Expenses

Regular, recurring costs that remain consistent each month, such as rent, mortgage payments, and insurance premiums. Fixed expenses are predictable and should be included in your budget.

Foreclosure

A legal process in which a lender takes possession of a property after the homeowner fails to make mortgage payments. Foreclosure can result in the loss of a home and damage to the homeowner's credit score.

401(k)

A tax-advantaged retirement savings plan offered by many employers. Contributions are made pre-tax, and the money grows tax-free until withdrawn in retirement. Many employers match a portion of employee contributions.

G

Gross Income

The total income earned before any taxes or deductions. Gross income includes wages, salaries, bonuses, and other sources of income, such as rental income or investment returns.

I

Index Fund

A type of mutual fund or ETF that aims to replicate the performance of a specific market index, such as the S&P 500. Index funds provide broad market exposure and tend to have lower fees than actively managed funds.

Inflation

The increase in prices of goods and services over time, which reduces the purchasing power of money. Inflation is typically measured by the Consumer Price Index (CPI).

Interest Rate

The percentage of a loan or deposit balance that is paid by the borrower to the lender (for loans) or earned by the saver (for deposits). Interest rates can be fixed or variable.

IRA (Individual Retirement Account)

A tax-advantaged retirement savings account that individuals can use to save for retirement. Traditional IRAs offer tax-deductible contributions, while Roth IRAs provide tax-free withdrawals in retirement.

L

Liability

A financial obligation or debt that an individual or company owes. Examples of liabilities include loans, credit card balances, and mortgages.

Liquidity

The ability to quickly convert an asset into cash without losing value. High-liquidity assets include cash, stocks, and bonds, while real estate and certain investments may be less liquid.

M

Mortgage

A loan used to purchase real estate, typically a home. The property serves as collateral for the loan, and the borrower repays the loan in regular installments over a set period (usually 15-30 years).

Mutual Fund

An investment vehicle that pools money from many investors to purchase a diversified portfolio of stocks, bonds, or other securities. Mutual funds are managed by professional portfolio managers.

N

Net Income

The amount of income left after taxes and other deductions have been subtracted from your gross income. Also known as take-home pay, net income is the amount you can use for savings, expenses, and investments.

Net Worth

The total value of your assets minus your liabilities. Net worth is a measure of your overall financial health and is calculated by subtracting what you owe (debts) from what you own (assets).

P

Principal

The original amount of money borrowed or invested, excluding any interest or earnings. When repaying a loan, the principal refers to the outstanding balance that must be repaid.

Profit and Loss Statement (P&L)

A financial statement that summarizes the revenues, costs, and expenses incurred during a specific period. It provides a snapshot of a company's financial performance, showing net profit or loss.

R

Recession

A period of economic decline characterized by a drop in gross domestic product (GDP), higher unemployment, and reduced consumer spending. Recessions can last for several months or years.

Roth IRA

A type of individual retirement account (IRA) where contributions are made after taxes, but qualified withdrawals in retirement are tax-free. Roth IRAs are ideal for individuals who expect to be in a higher tax bracket in the future.

S

Savings Account

A deposit account held at a bank or credit union that earns interest on the money saved. Savings accounts are low-risk and typically used for short-term goals or emergency funds.

Stock

A type of security that represents ownership in a company. When you buy a stock, you own a share of the company and may benefit from dividends and capital appreciation.

S&P 500

An index of 500 of the largest publicly traded companies in the U.S. It is widely used as a benchmark for the overall performance of the U.S. stock market.

T

Tax Deduction

An expense that reduces your taxable income, lowering the amount of taxes you owe. Common deductions include mortgage interest, charitable donations, and medical expenses.

Tax-Deferred

A tax benefit that allows you to postpone paying taxes on earnings until they are withdrawn, typically used in retirement accounts like 401(k)s and IRAs. Tax-deferred growth allows investments to compound without being taxed annually.

Term Life Insurance

A type of life insurance that provides coverage for a specified period (or "term"), such as 10, 20, or 30 years. If the policyholder dies during the term, the beneficiaries receive a death benefit.

W

Will

A legal document that outlines how a person's assets should be distributed after death. A will also designates guardians for minor children and can include instructions for settling debts and taxes.

Withholding

The portion of an employee's wages that an employer deducts for taxes and other obligations, such as Social Security and Medicare. Withholding helps ensure that taxes are paid throughout the year.

Conclusion

This glossary provides easy-to-understand definitions of the most important financial terms covered in the book. Use it as a reference whenever you encounter unfamiliar financial language or concepts. By improving your financial literacy, you'll be better equipped to make informed decisions and achieve your financial goals. Understanding these terms is a crucial step on your path to financial independence and long-term success.

<u>Message from the Author:</u>

I hope you enjoyed this book, I love astrology and knew there was not a book such as this out on the shelf. I love metaphysical items as well. Please check out my other books:

-Life of Government Benefits

-My life of Hell

-My life with Hydrocephalus

-Red Sky

-World Domination:Woman's rule

-World Domination:Woman's Rule 2: The War

-Life and Banishment of Apophis: book 1

-The Kidney Friendly Diet

-The Ultimate Hemp Cookbook

-Creating a Dispensary(legally)

-Cleanliness throughout life: the importance of showering from childhood to adulthood.

-Strong Roots: The Risks of Overcoddling children

-Hemp Horoscopes: Cosmic Insights and Earthly Healing

- Celestial Hemp Navigating the Zodiac: Through the Green Cosmos

-Astrological Hemp: Aligning The Stars with Earth's Ancient Herb

-The Astrological Guide to Hemp: Stars, Signs, and Sacred Leaves

-Green Growth: Innovative Marketing Strategies for your Hemp Products and Dispensary

-Cosmic Cannabis

-Astrological Munchies

-Henry The Hemp

-Zodiacal Roots: The Astrological Soul Of Hemp

- **Green Constellations: Intersection of Hemp and Zodiac**

-Hemp in The Houses: An astrological Adventure Through The Cannabis Galaxy

-Galactic Ganja Guide

Heavenly Hemp

Zodiac Leaves

Doctor Who Astrology

Cannastrology

Stellar Satvias and Cosmic Indicas

<u>Celestial Cannabis: A Zodiac Journey</u>

AstroHerbology: The Sky and The Soil: Volume 1

AstroHerbology:Celestial Cannabis:Volume 2

Cosmic Cannabis Cultivation

The Starry Guide to Herbal Harmony: Volume 1

The Starry Guide to Herbal Harmony: Cannabis Universe: Volume 2

Yugioh Astrology: Astrological Guide to Deck, Duels and more

Nightmare Mansion: Echoes of The Abyss

Nightmare Mansion 2: Legacy of Shadows

Nightmare Mansion 3: Shadows of the Forgotten

Nightmare Mansion 4: Echoes of the Damned

The Life and Banishment of Apophis: Book 2

Nightmare Mansion: Halls of Despair

<u>Healing with Herb: Cannabis and Hydrocephalus</u>

<u>Planetary Pot: Aligning with Astrological Herbs: Volume 1</u>

Fast Track to Freedom: 30 Days to Financial Independence Using AI, Assets, and Agile Hustles

<u>Cosmic Hemp Pathways</u>

How to Become Financially Free in 30 Days: 10,000 Paths to Prosperity

Zodiacal Herbage: Astrological Insights: Volume 1

Nightmare Mansion: Whispers in the Walls

The Daleks Invade Atlantis

Henry the hemp and Hydrocephalus

10X The Kidney Friendly Diet

Cannabis Universe: Adult coloring book

Hemp Astrology: The Healing Power of the Stars

Zodiacal Herbage: Astrological Insights: Cannabis Universe: Volume 2

<u>Planetary Pot: Aligning with Astrological Herbs: Cannabis Universes: Volume 2</u>

Doctor Who Meets the Replicators and SG-1: The Ultimate Battle for Survival

Nightmare Mansion: Curse of the Blood Moon

<u>The Celestial Stoner: A Guide to the Zodiac</u>

Cosmic Pleasures: Sex Toy Astrology for Every Sign

Hydrocephalus Astrology: Navigating the Stars and Healing Waters

Lapis and the Mischievous Chocolate Bar

Celestial Positions: Sexual Astrology for Every Sign

Apophis's Shadow Work Journal: : A Journey of Self-Discovery and Healing

Kinky Cosmos: Sexual Kink Astrology for Every Sign

Digital Cosmos: The Astrological Digimon Compendium

Stellar Seeds: The Cosmic Guide to Growing with Astrology

Apophis's Daily Gratitude Journal

Cat Astrology: Feline Mysteries of the Cosmos

The Cosmic Kama Sutra: An Astrological Guide to Sexual Positions

Unleash Your Potential: A Guided Journal Powered by AI Insights

Whispers of the Enchanted Grove

Cosmic Pleasures: An Astrological Guide to Sexual Kinks

369, 12 Manifestation Journal

Whisper of the nocturne journal(blank journal for writing or drawing)

The Boogey Book

Locked In Reflection: A Chastity Journey Through Locktober

Generating Wealth Quickly:

How to Generate $100,000 in 24 Hours

Star Magic: Harness the Power of the Universe

The Flatulence Chronicles: A Fart Journal for Self-Discovery

The Doctor and The Death Moth

Seize the Day: A Personal Seizure Tracking Journal

The Ultimate Boogeyman Safari: A Journey into the Boogie World and Beyond

Whispers of Samhain: 1,000 Spells of Love, Luck, and Lunar Magic: Samhain Spell Book

Apophis's guides:

Witch's Spellbook Crafting Guide for Halloween

<u>Frost & Flame: The Enchanted Yule Grimoire of 1000 Winter Spells</u>

<u>The Ultimate Boogey Goo Guide & Spooky Activities for Halloween Fun</u>

Harmony of the Scales: A Libra's Spellcraft for Balance and Beauty

The Enchanted Advent: 36 Days of Christmas Wonders

Nightmare Mansion: The Labyrinth of Screams

Harvest of Enchantment: 1,000 Spells of Gratitude, Love, and Fortune for Thanksgiving

The Boogey Chronicles: A Journal of Nightly Encounters and Shadowy Secrets

If you want solar for your home go here: https://www.harborso-lar.live/apophisenterprises/

Get Some Tarot cards: https://www.makeplayingcards.com/sell/apophis-occult-shop

Get some shirts: https://www.bonfire.com/store/apophis-shirt-emporium/

<u>Instagrams:</u>
@apophis_enterprises,
@apophisbookemporium,
@apophisscardshop
Twitter: @apophisenterpr1
 Tiktok:@apophisenterprise
Youtube: @sg1fan23477, @FiresideRetreatKingdom

Podcast: Apophis Chat Zone: https://open.spotify.com/show/
5zXbrCLEV2xzCp8ybrfHsk?si=fb4d4fdbdce44dec

Newsletter: https://apophiss-newsletter-27c897.beehiiv.com/